Contents

Introduction

John Lennon's song "Imagine" is the inspiration for this book. The first ten years of my life mimicked his lyrics to a high degree. In my travels and experience, I have found many other communities that are harmonious and peaceful. Growing up as I did should be available to all children. Moving in the direction of Lennon's lyrics is essential to begin cleaning up the environment so that our grandchildren do not experience the death of humanity.

The top red roof is the house where I was born

My first memory is watching my family's pig being slaughtered. I watched in fascination as the butcher's heavy mallet came down squarely on top of the tethered animal's head. Once confirmed dead, I helped spread straw on top and around the dead beast and lit the straw on fire. The pungent smell of hair and flesh burning filled the air. Once the flames expired, the butcher began separating the skin from the carcass, gutting the abdominal cavity and carving the rest in large sections, saving a quarter for himself. For the following two days, our family was busy dissecting, packing and making sausage from the carcass. The intestines made effective casings. The meat would easily last through the winter. It was 1948. I was 3.

We lived less than a kilometer from Lury-sur-Arnon, a town of about 600 in the Loire Valley farm country. Our small home sat on a hilltop overlooking the town and could be described generously as having three rooms of living space for the five of us. We did have a cellar where wine and canned preserves were stored and another barn-like storage area. A coal-burning stove dominated the living /kitchen area and I cannot possibly imagine it without my mother occupied at it, preparing meals. A room off the kitchen area held the beds where the family slept. We had no running water, electricity, TV, radio, telephone, or car. My parents did have bicycles. In other words, we had everything we needed.

My father began soldiering in his early teens. The Bolshevik Revolution began, then WWI and, by the end of that war, the family had enough money for his transport. However, he was also just old enough to be drafted by the Polish army. So, instead of using the money saved for transport, it was used to buy him out of the army. He decided to get a work permit to go to France as a miner in order to get out of Poland and the changing political environment. He would spend two years in French coal mines.

When he finished his contract, he was either convinced or connived into signing up for the French Foreign Legion. My father was not a very talkative person and never expanded on the facts, but the family in Chicago believes he was shanghaied. Regardless of the reason, his next five years would be spent in Morocco.

Ladislas (Walter) Stachura (1928)

The French Foreign Legion is known to be very, very tough. No French citizen can join it – that's why it's called what it's called. It is a last resort for a lot of different characters, many of whom do not care to discuss their past. Legendary discipline methods are used to remove individual character and build cohesive units. All members must learn to communicate in French and all that survive can become French citizens after their tenure in the

Legion. My dad became a member of a brotherhood that rivals any Special Forces unit now existing. He became a sergeant in his stint, which was unusual for five years of service. Many of his stories about forays into the desert, hand-to-hand battles and his pet monkey delighted me to the core. After his release, he settled in the small town I was born.

Lury-sur-Arnon, France

My father went to war again when World War Two started, but was captured and sent to a German prisoner of war camp. He escaped and spent the remainder of the war fighting in the underground resistance near our village. Rich, my oldest brother, was born in 1939, Mike, my older brother, was born in 1942, and I came along in 1944.

After the war, my mother had firmly made up her mind to bring her boys to the States. Communication with my dad's family restarted in earnest. My father traveled to Chicago in 1951 to see his family and returned to start the process of emigration.

My youthful years were totally blissful. I didn't know why rules existed, but I certainly didn't see them applying to me. I did what I wanted when I wanted and was what is usually referred to as a pain-in-the-ass. I participated in some group activities, but would much rather explore the river, woods and surrounding area by myself. I started school at three years old and was soon reading. My Christmas presents consisted of one or two new books and a sweater or some socks my mom had knitted. I don't recall ever receiving toys as a gift.

Mom tried to settle me down by giving me chores as soon as I was old enough. When I woke up in the morning, she would send me to the well to get water for coffee and breakfast. I would then check the chicken coops for eggs and bring them to the kitchen. Then, the rabbit hutches would be checked for availability of food. After coffee and bread, I would get 25 francs for the evening bread and head off to school. Many times, after I had experienced the aroma of the bakery and headed home with the loaf, I couldn't help but dig out the warm dough and would wind up at home with an empty crust. After my beating, I would be sent back to get a new loaf.

Beatings were administered by my mother with a cat-o-nine-tails. They were painful. One of these episodes was particularly memorable.

One winter was severe enough to freeze the surface of the river at the base of the hill. Being the way I am, I was fascinated by the ice spanning from bank to bank. I had never seen that before. I ventured onto the ice gingerly and felt the ice hold near the bank. Gathering courage, I eased forward with the intent of reaching the opposing bank. Near the middle, cracking sounds made me stop. Looking down, I saw leaves passing under the surface of the ice. I decided to ease back to my starting point. What I hadn't noticed was the parish priest looking down at me from the hilltop. When my mother got home from work, she administered the absolute best pain I ever felt. So, I did the only thing I could do – I tossed the cat-o-nine-tails into the outhouse. She had to resort to my father's belt for future beatings.

One of the chores I did not really care for was fetching my father from the town bar to bring him home for dinner. He took a train daily to his job in a porcelain factory in Vierzon. Other men from the town also worked there and would gather at the Hotel du Boeuf after work for a few glasses of wine. Some time prior to dinner being ready, my mom would dispatch me to bring him home. If he had too many snorts, I readied myself to play peacekeeper when we returned.

After he returned from visiting Chicago, my parents considered the move for the family. I think my dad really enjoyed his life in our little town and was reluctant to move into a big city. Until he left in August 1954 to get a job and apartment for us, there were many arguments. He even tossed the emigration papers in the stove fire during one of them. My mom had to reach into the flames to retrieve them. She persisted in her efforts to give her kids a better life.

My joy came from the wonderful environment of country living. Spring was fantastic - blossoms all over the place, farmers plowing their fields trailing their Percheron horses, our cherry trees in bloom, planting our garden, etc. My curiosity took me everywhere. Because we had no toys or money, we had to be creative to amuse ourselves. Spring and summer were all about creative joy.

Summertime was best. We would go fishing in the river, participate in endless cop-and-robber games with the town kids, play soccer, etc. The fruit trees around our house were constantly under siege for their prized product. Cherries, pears, apples, plums and garden produce went directly from Mother Earth to our bellies or in jars for the winter. I never saw any food in a box or tin can until we reached Chicago. I spent many nights reclining on the hillside, looking at a sky filled with stars.

Harvest time was also joyful. The entire town would participate with the farmers in bringing the crops in. We had two small vineyards my dad harvested to make wine for the year. Neighbors would help him and we would help neighbors until all the work was done. Three days of festivities would end the harvest.

These first ten years of my life gave me a foundation that is still with me. Growing up without electricity, indoor plumbing, television, radio, toys or money was the best thing that could happen to any child. We lived in total harmony with nature and neighbors.

Fifty-eight years later, things are much different. The population of the world has doubled; the planet is being ravaged by greed and corruption; and there is a chance we may not be able to stop our insanity soon enough to reverse the process of suicide. We must wake up and take control of our destiny away from the politicians. That means taking individual responsibility for our actions.

I began programming computers in 1963 at the age of eighteen. I researched for many years and I have investigated hundreds of business systems in my sales career. In 1995, I met Paul. He and I created Cognitor, Inc. to market a product we named Cogitator, or thinker. It is the tool that can be used to reach John Lennon's ideal world. In short, it separates intelligence from knowledge in a computer and "thinks" about what it needs to do next. Paul and I will soon mark our fiftieth year since we began programming - we know

Cogitator's potential. It is currently doing fantastic work at the Chicago Transit Police and is targeting Medicare fraud to the tune of 25 to 50 billion dollars savings to the system this year. We ousted IBM consultants in both cases. Here is my presentation slide:

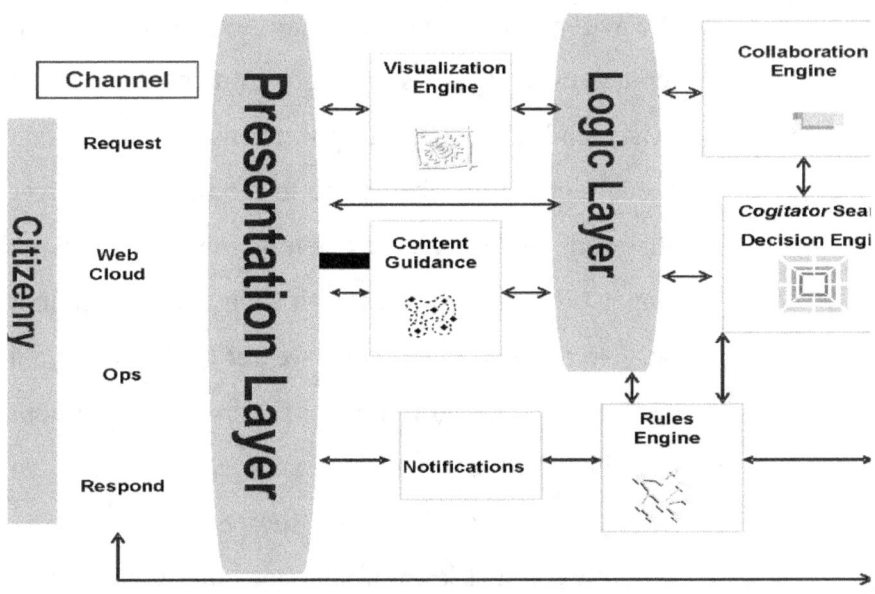

At the core of the system is the Cogitator inference and decision engine

If you are familiar with Star Trek, you know that Captain Picard of the Enterprise talks to the computer and the computer answers him. Cogitator can make that happen for everyone, regardless of language. The technology is here now. The difference is that Cogitator would be available to all the communities and individuals of John Lennon's song. Self-governing is possible today.

We will refer to this schematic as needed. It can replace every business and government system that exists and eliminate all politicians and corporate executives. It has the ability to monitor and deliver all goods and services to every individual on the planet. It communicates with each user and cannot lie. No more secrets. How we get to that state in a non-violent progression of changes without negatively affecting anyone and causing panic in the ignorant is the way the puzzle must be assembled. Just know for certain that this concept is already working. Getting us to Lennon's ideal world is not only through teaching Cogitator, but also by unlearning false beliefs and values. There will be resistance. The reason to move forward in this direction is serious.

Pollution and global warming are destroying our grandchildren's future. We are an endangered species, along with most other organic life forms. We must change and adapt or die. We must live as one or die as a group.

One Community Design for John Lennon's
Vision

Puzzle Pieces

If we are to be living in the world of "Imagine," there are many elements of today's culture that need to be eliminated or prioritized differently. In fact, a huge paradigm shift of consciousness will have to occur in the population in achieving world peace and "living as one." It may take a generation or more to make the shift to sanity due to the ingrained habits of the older segment of the population. The unifying factor is the power of the World Wide Web. If enough world citizens agree to purge their indoctrination and false beliefs, it may happen more quickly. Those who cannot or will not adapt will merely follow or fade into history.

One definition of democracy is "the control of an organization by its members, who have a free and equal right to participate in decision-making processes." This is the definition needed to create Lennon's vision. Because communities will have autonomy to a large extent, once the basic needs of the individuals are met, choices can be made to create the kind of environment the majority prefers.

The basics are food, shelter, clothing and safety. They will be the priority for Cogitator to manage from the Internet Cloud. Additional requests and requirements of the community members will be prioritized according to the voting of the group.

Mobility among communities will eventually be wide open to those who want to mingle with those of similar values and activities. The only caveat is that there must be appropriate space for those wishing to make a change. Communities will be limited to a certain population to not affect their ability to be self-sustaining, but new communities will be established as they become necessary. It will take some time to create a balanced mix, but, eventually, individuals and families will be able to live anywhere in the world in the environment of their choice. There will be no countries, therefore, no borders. Borders simply create conflict.

These communities will assign responsibility to each individual for only two functions – taking care of the planet and taking care of each other. Virtually all manufacturing and distribution logistics for needed goods and services will be managed by Cogitator automatically. There will be need for human participation in automated factories and the movement of goods, but there would be plenty of volunteers who can perform these tasks. The jobs can certainly be shared equitably among those with the required skills and abilities.

All education will be free and open to everyone. Children will not be taught what to learn, but how to learn. Nature will take care of the development of each individual for whatever talents each is born with. This will undoubtedly lead to creativity in both science and art. The Universe is constantly expanding and adapting in ways that are not yet fully understood by our human ability, but that does not mean that will remain a mystery.

The physical work required for maintaining communities and producing food will be shared equitably. Each home will have access to Cogitator's Knowledge Base to determine the day's needs to maintain the environment. Any functions needing attention will be contained in a "Job Jar" for the members to fulfill. Those wishing to take a proactive approach will be able to take responsibility for needed functions by simply verbally telling Cogitator which tasks they want. Since all major languages can be converted to voice recognition, it would not matter what part of the world a community is located – all community members could communicate in their native language.

Specialized functions would be assigned to the proper skill set from historical activity and a "resume" file. Competency would be recorded based on the results of completed tasks. Carpenters, electricians, plumbers, farmers, teachers and the like would develop through experience from Beginner through Master ratings. Airplane pilots, train engineers, truck drivers, technical personnel and such would be rated similarly. Artists and scientists could collaborate and share their creativity to provide a better world for its citizens. In fact, artists and scientists should be the primary sources of leadership.

Once stabilized, communities would have little work to do. Group and individual activities would be available to interested participants. Sports, games, amusement or gatherings to share experiences would be created by the communities for participation by all. Since money would no longer exist, no professional sports would be available, but teams could play any sport voluntarily under Olympic-type rules. Amusement could be plays, motion pictures, and anything related to the arts. Television and radio would be used for music, the arts, education and information purposes only.

Violence would be outlawed in every form of activity. Justice would be administered by ending communication with the offenders until a resolution was reached or a forced removal from the community would be decided. Silence can be a very strong motivator. Leaders would be necessary to some extent, but only to provide wisdom, maintain safety and develop relationships with other communities for mutual benefit.

Different types of communities would be designed. Some would perform services for outsiders, some would produce food, provide facilities for tourism, maintain historical sites, build new communities, etc. All functions and privileges would be prioritized by Cogitator according to needs first, then wants, and finally by merit. If requests for privileges outnumber the availability of slots, they will be filled first with those who participate most in community support. All requests would eventually be served.

Initially, if not forever, some people will choose to live outside communities. There are many who can live on their own without community support. This is totally acceptable. The real reason for community living is to do away with the centralized control exercised on cities by the Plutarchy. Since there will be no money, crime will seldom occur and most probably not within a community. Additionally, facilities for travelers will always be available to anyone who wants to pass time in any community. Freedom is the objective, but it must come with responsibility for all.

Ultimately, every citizen will have access to the entire knowledge base monitored by Cogitator. Additionally, all communication can be person-to-person among all users of the system, as well as serving all needs for day-to-day living. It is absolutely essential that a worldwide union of people who want to protect the earth become active in resisting the Plutarchy. As Gandhi proved, no power can withstand the will of the people. We must return to sanity.

Initially, there needs to be a foundation within the existing system for world citizens to unify their efforts. Until the time of eliminating money completely, there has to be commingling of functions between the existing infrastructure and the people of Occupy Earth. This can be done by establishing a Bank of Gaea or some similar financial institution that can accept deposits from all those who want to become world citizens. This should send a strong message to the Plutarchy by draining some of their monetary power. Temporarily, the funds deposited can be used for transitioning to community-based governance.

Companies that want to participate in this movement will receive free services to manage their business. Transactions will be processed and reports generated as required by current law and taxes will be paid automatically at no cost to them. This service would be a huge advantage in reducing cost of goods sold against competition. Eventually, these companies will only accept Bank of Gaea "authorized" cards to receive payments. That means that people who want to do business with these firms will have to open an account with the

Bank of Gaea. There are millions of small companies compared to few corporate giants. Local businesses will thrive and overseas jobs will disappear. We will have begun our dependence on each other instead of money.

The exodus from big cities will begin in earnest. Thousands of small towns that were losing population due to the attraction of money and thrills in large cities will now be sought out as places of peace and tranquility. The Bank of Gaea will loan the money required by green developers to build more housing in the surrounding rural landscape. The old infrastructure will erode faster and faster as more and more money is spent in community economies. As more and more millions join the movement around the world and refuse to serve the Plutarchy, politicians will no longer have any power. When the time is ripe, all payment of taxes will stop. As more population localizes and green energy is used, usage of oil will drop until the price of a gallon of gas is less than a dollar. The

Plutarchy will no longer be able to manipulate the population. Money will disappear.

This will perhaps happen without conflict, but that's doubtful. Removing power from the Plutarchy is certainly simple enough, but only by worldwide participation can we end war and destruction of the planet. It is very important to realize that those who will make this happen is not from the majority of sheep that follow whomever in power. This will be the layer of middle and upper-middle class individuals who have already realized that current leaders are not the ones who will aid in creating John Lennon's vision. Unfortunately, the sheep still get to vote. That is the holdup to peace – ignorance.

One great benefit from this move is the huge intellectual collateral that will become available from financial industries, jurisprudence, defense and other wasteful endeavors. These additional human resources can be retrained to contribute real value to the new system. The millions of techies now occupied doing support work for the Plutarchy will be taught how to convert existing infrastructures to the World Wide Web and tyranny will die soon after. It is a fact that the Plutarchy would not exist without controlling automation. The techies are the true power today.

When I started programming in 1963, no standardization existed. Since then, standardization has allowed technocrats to absorb less capable organizations. It is the standardization of cultural thinking that can change the world. The standardization of The Community System is necessary.

Systematization

All systems work exactly the same way is the first understanding we must make to create a new system. That is, all systems need <u>input</u> to <u>process</u> and create the desired <u>output</u>. Our language reflects this with every sentence as subject(s), verb and object(s). The output is our objective. Verbs are <u>action</u> words. If we take no action, we have no output.

All systems are interconnected is the next understanding. We have unlimited access to everything that exists in one way or another. Finding the input to create a system objective is similar to getting the ingredients for a recipe to make a meal.

In making a meal, once we have our ingredients and our objective in mind, we apply a methodology to those ingredients. That method is like the recipe instructions in the **order of execution** necessary for the meal to turn out successfully. This is a program, routine or app. There are many recipes to create a specific meal. Depending upon the skill, expertise, tools and attentiveness of the chef, the same recipe will yield different results. No meal will ever be duplicated exactly. Individual preferences will enter into the mix, temperatures may vary, etc.

In a computer however, we only deal with ones and zeroes in cyberspace. The apps we give it are streams of human thought converted to binary so that the machine can perform tasks that can be automated. Witness the loss of jobs since the advent of computers. We get much more accurate and effective results from computers than from people with personal preferences.

We have recipes for everything we do in daily activities. Whether taking a shower, driving to work, making love, golfing, ad infinitum, no person does anything exactly the same way as anyone else. We are like snowflakes.

Technology appears quite complex to the average person, but it's only a tool. Computers are extensions of the human brain, specifically, the left hemisphere. We don't need to know how the computer is put together to be a user, but we should know its potential. The intelligence required to understand today's technology is not really that much, if we reduce it to its lowest common denominator.

The lowest common denominator that runs the whole shebang is 1 and the absence of 1 – zero. From this binary nature, all systems are created, including our own. It is the sequential arrangement of these two elements that can translate all human thought into machine instructions. All programs are congealed thoughts in electronic form. Indeed, the word "information" can be stated as thoughts *in formation*, like a military unit. A soldier is a datum, or 1, a unit is data in formation, a regiment is more information linked together, etc. If we can agree that sequences of zeroes and ones are the basis for all systems existing in the world today we can agree that they can be modified.

Computerization began in the middle of the nineteenth century. George Boole and Charles Babbage were trying to bring a concept into life called the Difference Engine. Boole wrote "The Calculus of Logic" and "Laws of Thought" which define how people process thoughts and make decisions, mostly in formulaic depictions. Boolean Logic is the core of all programming. In that work, it is obvious that a thought is a cycle, not a thing. Roughly stated, it follows the path of Awareness, Focus, Recognition, Interest and Action to create the next thought cycle. The more interest we have in what we behold, the more thought cycles we go through before taking any action. Boole also made us aware of the binary numbering system. All numbering systems other than binary are artificial and do not exist in truth. Since then, communication and connectivity has exploded to a point where we are approaching mental telepathy.

Today, voice recognition, Global Positioning System, Internet, instant communication anywhere on the globe all contribute to our potential for change. We've gone from trepanning and leeching to microsurgery. We cannot use any credit cards without information being gathered by the issuer. We can't go through an automated toll gate without recording location and time. Speeding tickets can be issued if we get to the next gate too fast. Most factories contain a few technicians and a robotic population. In the fifty years since I began programming, the world has completely changed. We're already at breakneck pace and still speeding up. Where are we going?

Computers also allow us to extend our physical senses. The Hubble telescope is one example of how we can see far and the electronic microscope sees deep into molecular structures. The Maracaibo antenna "listens" for messages from deep space continually. We can converse with astronauts millions of miles away and send instructions to

Mars probes. Truly wondrous abilities! All are controlled with sequences of zeroes and ones.

Technology today is pretty much used to control people's actions, moods, as well as thoughts. If we come to realize that we as a group can use technology for the betterment of life on Earth, we must have a plan. A somewhat simple plan, so that everyone can see the benefit. Technology may be daunting to some, but not to Cogitator. It is daunting to the ignorant, though.

My experience is mostly in corporate systems and I am quite familiar with their structure. Their systems are designed much the same way the human body is. Indeed, "corpus" means body in Latin. A corporation is an artificial body. Its General Ledger is the heart. This corporate heart controls cash flow, our heart controls blood flow. The brain is the executive level; organs like liver, stomach, lungs, etc, are the various departments that execute functions related to keeping the body healthy. A healthy body is in balance. A healthy corporation balances Assets and Liabilities and excretes profits.

I started imagining how I could put technology to work in an "ideal" company. Many of my friends and associates work at home and really like it. No travel time, no gasoline usage, freedom of working hours, etc. Their physical presence at some cubicle is not necessary to perform their duties. We already have a connection to cyberspace in reading this. Why not use it as a group to maintain our communities in the way we all desire? After Paul and I founded Cognitor and started marketing Cogitator, I visualized a new way to do things without destroying the planet.

The problem with traditional programs is maintenance. Every time something new comes along, change must be effected in the program, sometimes by a programmer other than the originator, which has the potential of creating more problems. Another big issue is that the huge number of coded lines in most companies' systems.

Cogitator could eliminate more than 90% of those lines. Using reusable code and putting the programs together as needed eliminates redundancy and maintenance. Changes are made to the knowledge bases, not the programming.

The system works with Knowledge Bases. This is where the data and their relationships are kept. If you are aware of knowledge-based systems, you know that this not simply data storage. We can compare these to our human memory. When we make plans to achieve a goal, we use our memory and previous experiences to activate a procedure to make it happen. Knowledge bases contain know-what, know-when and know-how to activate functions and procedures to process input into output.

Some people ask if this is Artificial Intelligence. There is no such thing. Artificial means man-made. Our Satanic Ego is the only man-made intelligence. True intelligence is innate in all forms. The artificial part of decision-making is the knowledge.

Intelligence works with knowledge to create wisdom. If the knowledge is tainted with false beliefs and values, the system will not work properly. That's how our society got all fouled up. It must be debugged.

Another asset of Paul's software is that it can "learn." After the conversion of existing systems to one of Intelligence/Knowledge, whenever it encounters a new stimulus (transaction,) it seeks to compare it to what it "knows" to determine if it is only a variation of a similar transaction. Before making the decision, it will communicate with a human with its findings. If the human makes the decision, it "remembers" and will avoid asking again when the same transaction returns.

After a couple of years of trying to get this company off the ground, I gave up. All the meetings we had resulted in spotty work that never established the potential. The executives we approached were of two kinds- those who could not imagine the concept and those who understood that this system would remove the need for executives. The second kind did not want to download their knowledge for the computer to get better results than they themselves could provide.

I turned my efforts to debugging the human system, starting with my own. There is no way anyone can know someone else better than oneself, so that's what I set out to do. Get to know me completely, not in the sense of who I am, but *what* I am. I discovered that we are spiritual beings experiencing a human life. After studying Einstein's Special Theory of Relativity and its successor, Quantum Mechanics, I found the counterpart to zeroes and ones in humans - Wave/Particle. Zero is the wave and one is the particle. The same equation proves the existence of both. This is why computers are able to do so much. Whatever we think can be converted to zeroes and ones.

All computer systems are controlled by an operating system, whether UNIX, Jaguar, or any other. They work the same way ours does. The difference is that they need to be connected to the elements they use to stay in balance. As evidenced today, the connections can be expanded indefinitely into all walks of life. From Washington, D.C. down to and through each worker, the connections are there. The key to each level is the social security number and the tax ID number. That's our economic system. It requires debugging.

The method for returning this planet to the heaven it was is in our hands. We have to return to self-sustaining communities and connect to all other self-sustaining communities. The Internet can make this a reality. All existing systems of products, services and logistics already reside on computers. The conversion to a knowledge base may seem daunting, but we have an automated way to convert code into knowledge from existing programming. The effort would be minimal if the existing workforce would participate. They could be trained quickly enough. None of the existing systems would suffer because functions and programs would be converted piecemeal and the system would use both old and new technology until fully converted. Once that is underway, it is a matter of segmenting society into communities in an ever growing spiral that eventually would be united in a new world order - John Lennon's "Imagine."

Standardization

I have been solving puzzles ever since I arrived in this country and I see the current State of the World as a huge picture puzzle. Right now, we have before us a huge pile of pieces to form the "Big Picture," but we lost the cover of the box the pieces came in. There are also puzzle pieces from other pictures that do not belong to the one we want to create. This will be an attempt to at least start putting the pieces together. We must first agree on the goal – living life in peace according to John Lennon's song. We can draw the Big Picture together, but we must have some ground rules in doing so to create the best picture we can.

The implication of that song implies that many changes to our current systems need be made. Having grown up during the age of meaningful lyrics, being a Vietnam veteran and watching protests against the machine we call The System compels me to communicate how we may head for that ideal world. We must address our beliefs, values and political systems and attempt to remove all false and incomplete puzzle pieces. We must communicate the truth.

Ground Rules

My own rules for communicating with others come from "The Four Agreements" by Don Miguel de Ruiz. The agreements are:

Be Impeccable with your Word

Speak with integrity. Say only what you mean. Avoid using the words to speak against your self or to gossip about others. Use the power of your Word in the direction of truth and love. We can handle the worst Truth much more easily than the best lie. It is a waste of energy to spend time on what is not true.

Don't Take Anything Personally

Nothing others do is because of you. What others say and do is a projection of their own reality, their own dream. When you are immune to the opinions and actions of others, you won't be the victim of needless suffering. Forgive their ignorance and say: "I love you anyway."

Don't Make Assumptions

Find the courage to ask questions and to express what you really want. Every belief we have is just an assumption. We must question our beliefs and communicate with others as clearly as we can to avoid misunderstandings, sadness and drama. With just this one agreement, we can completely transform our life.

Always Do Your Best

Our best is going to change from moment to moment; it will be different when we are healthy as opposed to sick. Under any circumstance, simply do our best and we will avoid self-judgment, self-abuse, and regrets.

These principles were added to in "The Fifth Agreement,"

Listen With Intent

If we agree to communicate with these principles in mind, we will achieve a much higher level of understanding and cooperation together. Communication is defined as: "The sending or receiving of a message that _**means the same**_ to both sender and receiver." There is little chance of that happening if we do not use the agreements stated above. Ground Rule Number One for standardization of communication is the usage of the five agreements.

The next thing we need to agree on is what we use to communicate with each other. You are using your eyes to read these words and formulating a picture within your mind. I am here and you are there and yet, you can imagine what these alphabetic characters mean to you. Pretty cool! If I were to speak these words to you in person, it would be your hearing that would convey the meaning.

Helen Keller was blind and deaf and wrote fourteen books using her sense of touch only. She graduated from Radcliffe with honors and wrote her autobiography at age 24. There are multiple ways to communicate the same message. Miss Keller would surely agree that everything she "saw" was *in her mind*. It is the same for us. Ground Rule Number Two is that everything we can sense is seen in our mind for interpretation. There is no "outside."

Helen Keller

Our next agreement is to realize that nothing can exist without being connected to everything else, including ourselves. There is no life or substance that can exist in the Universe separate from it. That is Ground Rule Number Three.

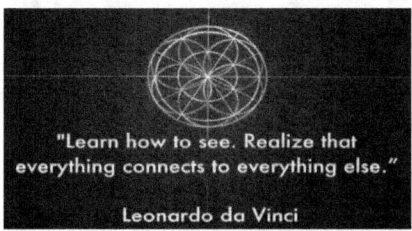

"Learn how to see. Realize that everything connects to everything else."

Leonardo da Vinci

While doing systems design and selling software to the Fortune 500, I realized that all corporations interact for their mutual benefit. All their systems are interconnected and all submit their results to government. From the smallest Mom and Pop operations to the largest conglomerate, all report to the same entity. All employees of those commercial enterprises are subsets (or cogs in the wheel) that work to create profit from their labors. They are the bricks in the pyramid depicted on the Great Seal of the United States.

ANNUIT CCEPTIS is loosely translated to "Providence has smiled upon us," and NOVUS ORDO SECLORUM means "New World Order."

It certainly doesn't appear that Providence has smiled upon the average person. I am for a New World Order that follows the John Lennon song, but that is not what is happening today. Our current leadership seems to be leading us on a path of destruction that should not be ignored. Who are these people?

How can our politicians not address issues that are critical to the planet and all its inhabitants before any other issues? If they are aliens trying to build interstellar craft in Area 52, that would make sense. This idea is made even more possible by the fact that trying to access information about this is blocked. If they are the Illuminati who know life is eternal, that would make sense. If either is true, why would this necessitate causing so much pain to the ignorant? The politicians themselves must be ignorant or totally insane, regardless of purpose. They must be identified and questioned. We should not be building surveillance systems and drones to watch citizens – they should be used to watch politicians.

I have combined Plutocracy and Oligarchy to coin the word "Plutarchy." Plutocracy means "government by the rich" and oligarchy means "government by the few" and that is the political condition we live under. In mythology, Pluto was the god of the underworld and its riches, ergo plutocracy. Plutarchy identifies the group in charge pretty well. Under the guise of "National Security," the Plutarchy has designed security systems to protect them from those being governed.

Institutions, governments, or any group that tries to separate from others are the sole danger to this planet. However, society and any group within it are supported by their members. Ground Rule Four is that we are individually responsible for supporting any group. Collectively, we can eliminate any power structure that does not serve all of us well and equitably.

The power of boycotts, strikes, protests and civil disobedience is undeniable if enough people are willing to participate. There is no need for violence. Mahatma Gandhi proved that.

Before people are willing to participate though, they must understand why. They must have a cause to rouse their minds from hypnosis. That only happens with new knowledge and understanding. Most people don't do anything to participate because they don't know what to do and some because they don't care. What's the difference between ignorance and apathy? – Don't know; don't care! These types are the ones allowing bad leadership to thrive through their ignorance.

The Plutarchy uses many techniques to manage its herds. Some herds are identified as countries and some are identified as religions. To unify the world per Lennon, both of these must be eliminated. We must identify the puzzle pieces that do not belong to the Big Picture and cast them aside. The Plutarchy also divides and conquers by creating opposing sides that compete for what they think is best. Liberals and conservatives are a good example.

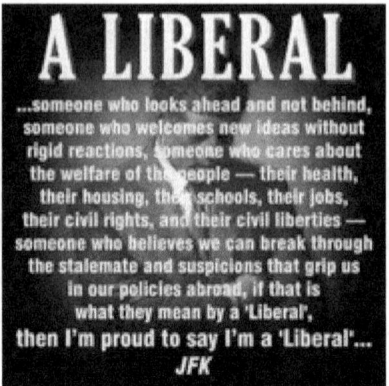

A LIBERAL
...someone who looks ahead and not behind, someone who welcomes new ideas without rigid reactions, someone who cares about the welfare of the people — their health, their housing, their schools, their jobs, their civil rights, and their civil liberties — someone who believes we can break through the stalemate and suspicions that grip us in our policies abroad, if that is what they mean by a 'Liberal', then I'm proud to say I'm a 'Liberal'...
JFK

This thought from John Kennedy may be why the Plutarchy killed him. My first day as a computer programmer was the day after his assassination. The world cried. Many great quotes from great people can be found on my boards at Pinterest.

The Plutarchy strives very hard to keep people ignorant and confused. This is the best way to foment fear. We do not fear what we know and the Plutarchy is aware that truth would set us free. The only way to remove fear is to remove ignorance. Educating ourselves is Ground Rule Number Five.

Virtually all mass media is controlled by the Plutarchy. Radio networks like Clear Channel, television networks like FOX, and most other networks spew edited versions of truth in their broadcasts and attempt to keep people confused and at odds with each other. Rupert Murdoch runs a huge media empire well known for its shady tactics.

TELEVISION

It's Called Programming For A Reason.

www.dollarvigilante.com

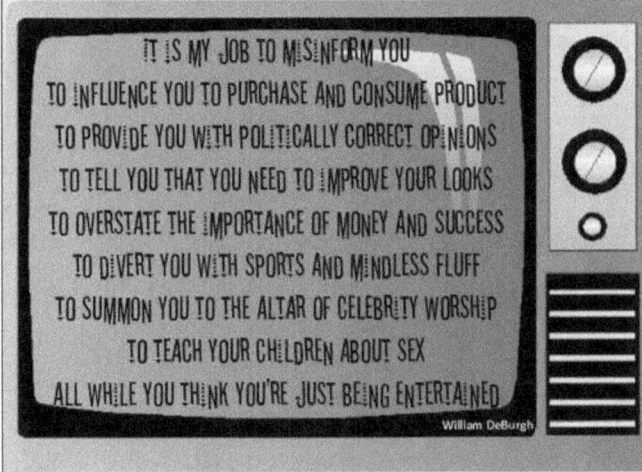

IT IS MY JOB TO MISINFORM YOU
TO INFLUENCE YOU TO PURCHASE AND CONSUME PRODUCT
TO PROVIDE YOU WITH POLITICALLY CORRECT OPINIONS
TO TELL YOU THAT YOU NEED TO IMPROVE YOUR LOOKS
TO OVERSTATE THE IMPORTANCE OF MONEY AND SUCCESS
TO DIVERT YOU WITH SPORTS AND MINDLESS FLUFF
TO SUMMON YOU TO THE ALTAR OF CELEBRITY WORSHIP
TO TEACH YOUR CHILDREN ABOUT SEX
ALL WHILE YOU THINK YOU'RE JUST BEING ENTERTAINED

William DeBurgh

These media are used to convince people to spend money on things they don't need with money they don't have to feed the coffers of the Plutarchy. The Plutarchy has extensive knowledge of hypnotic and subliminal techniques to achieve their ends. Television is the one-eyed hypnotist for our vision and radio hypnotizes us through our hearing. Newspapers take our attention from important issues by publishing vapid and inane articles in our local area to remind us how much crime and corruption we live among. The first boycott to be organized should be to turn off the mass media and start learning on our own and from each other. That would be Ground Rule Number six.

To recap our Ground Rules:

1) Communicate using The Five Agreements
2) Know that we only experience life INSIDE OUR MIND
3) Everything in the Universe is connected
4) Individuals have the power to refuse supporting any group
5) Education is the only way to improve ourselves

6) Ignore mass media messages from the Plutarchy

Self-Understanding

There is no way we can understand others better than we understand ourselves. It is by knowing WHAT we are and how we process the information that we sense from our environment that allows us to "change our minds." We must each understand WHY we do what we do before we stop doing anything. The more we understand ourselves, the more we understand others. As mentioned earlier with Helen Keller's life, we all see our environment in our minds, not "outside." This is a realization that must be understood to gain control of our actions. It is the first step towards removing ignorance.

Aside from the five physical senses, there are intangible senses. There are senses that live within us and help us through human experiences. They are Sense of Being, Sense of Balance, Sense of Sequence, Sense of Purpose and Sense of Love.

Sense of Being is universal in all creation. All things manifest themselves to us because they have a sense of being. All languages have a verb that signifies "to be." One of the questions all human beings eventually face is 'To be or not to be.' This sense is not exclusive to human beings. It creates the desire to exist and is the primary value of our lives as well as in all animals and plants. All actions and activities we perform are prioritized below this desire to have Being, or to live.

Sense of Balance also exists in all creation. When we were small and not yet walking, we attempted to stand on our own two feet and, eventually, we did. That was our sense of balance helping. It also senses the condition of your body to keep it in what is called homeostasis, which means "a balanced State of Being." It keeps our hearts beating at about seventy-two beats per minute, it monitors blood cells to remove carbon dioxide and replace it with oxygen. That oxygen burns the carbon-based food we eat – that's how we get energy to move our bodies. Suffice it to say that Sense of Balance is there to tell us when we need to adjust our behavior and regain balance.

Sense of Sequence is what allows us to know the order in which to execute the necessary steps for regaining balance. If we do thing out of sequence, we suffer the con-sequences. It performs the Process of Becoming (coming to be more than before). As Balance helps us make adjustments to stay in homeostasis, we evolve from the execution of those adjustments during the Process of Becoming. The DNA molecule in each of us contains two strands, one is the sequence of how to build the body we inhabit and the other has to instructions for completing each step of growth while maintaining Balance. That molecule is how we get our sense of sequence.

Sense of Purpose is our "raison d'être," the reason for our Being. We are all born to express the reason we came into the world. Stress and unhappiness come into our lives because we are not serving the purpose we were born to achieve. We probably will not know our purpose until we try any number of endeavors. This sense allows us to set goals (voluntary purposes) that may differ from our true purpose – like being a wage slave. We will know what that true purpose is when the joy of doing something that serves it makes our heart sing. We should follow our dream.

Sense of Love is what gives us the feeling that we all belong together and live as an extended family. It is a sharing of all creation for mutual appreciation. This Universal Love, or Agape, has no attachments to anything or anyone, because it knows that everything is connected as a unified whole. Genders exist to form unions between male and female to propagate our species. This love is Familial and Neighborly Love, includes all other life forms and comes second only to Universal Love. All other emotions are invalid, illusory and created by ignorance.

Sense of duty, sense of honor, sense of pride, sense of guilt, sense of fear, sense of anxiety and other such senses are all imposed on the human ego from societal programming and do not exist in Truth, only in the ego. The ego itself is a fabrication (an artificial mind) and is the source of all worldly ills. It creates false ideas to value, like Satan, Santa, sin and guilt, which do not exist in Truth. Ego creates a Personality, or identity. Personality comes from the Greek *persona*, which means mask. It is the self-defense mechanism the ego hides behind. It judges. Because it judges with false values and beliefs, it impedes recognition and understanding of our true being.

Becoming aware of why we do what we do is how we can make breakthroughs to our true being and our true purpose. If we question our actions and our words according to the five agreements, we can start peeling away the layers of deception and self-denial. As we see more and more of the truth of what we are, we can see the same in others and unite to create a better life for all. It is the aggregation of such people that can lead to John Lennon's vision. With these rules in mind, we can start organizing the puzzle pieces.

Personality

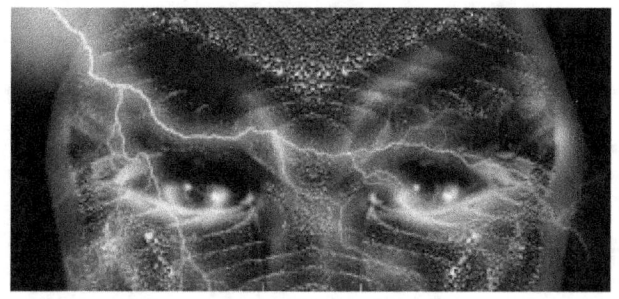

"The image and character that someone wants to show the outside world." Carl Jung.

"For imagination sets the goal picture which our automatic mechanism works on. We act, or fail to act, not because of will, as is so commonly believed, but because of imagination."

(We must imagine the end product of John Lennon's "Imagine" before we can achieve it)

"Realizing that our actions, feelings and behavior are the result of our own images and beliefs gives us the level that psychology has always needed for changing personality." - Maxwell Maltz

We all communicate our being, both to the outer and inner world we imagine. We are the only creatures who lie and accept lies as true. Why do we? We are the only creatures who get embarrassed, feel anger, judge others, and a whole lot more of seven deadly sins kind of behavior. What is this proud thing called ego and when will it regain its proper position in our lives?

Ego is an artificial structure built by human interaction and experience while treading the planet. It resides in the human brain in the form of memories. Its primary purpose is to monitor balance, or homeostasis, for our body, but it begins to build its own existence in us. Its real purpose is to use our physical senses to navigate through our human life. However, it goes beyond his job description by amassing beliefs and values from experience in society. It becomes a self-appointed judge. Not only does this judge provide sentencing of others, but it also judges our true being. It tries to maintain control by creating the illusion of guilt.

It uses the unique human trait of emotion to achieve this control.

 Edgar D. Mitchell, Apollo 14 astronaut and founder of the Institute for Noetic Sciences:

"The simple secret of the Universe if that you create your own reality."

In order to protect its sensitivity, ego builds protective armor in the form of masks, or veils. It becomes the gatekeeper that prevents new knowledge from eroding its control. The unfortunate part for this ego is that the universe is constantly expanding and all mind sets, if unwilling to grow, will eventually disappear into insignificance. We don't want to kill the ego. We need it to find food when we're hungry, a bed when we need rest, and a job when we're broke. It just has to understand that it is secondary to our real self. When it makes that realization, it becomes a friend and ally. Ego actually enjoys its role once we understand it. We all want to be understood.

The following poem was posted on the FanStory site on May 1, 2011. There are many segments on the site related to my book. It was originally written for Poetry.com and was published as the first page of their 2005 book of poems.

Ah! Dreaded Ego!

Ego craves for humanity
The true me wants divinity
It's bad enough to work and slave
Ego worries about the grave

It doesn't get Infinity
Has no clue of Eternity
Tries to create Identity
Please go to sleep Nonentity

If Truth be known, we are endless
Only Past dies, that's a promise
The future comes as we decide
So, come Ego, enjoy the ride

Whenever ego is our partner rather than our judge, new vistas open for our human endeavors. We can put it to work on our behalf and it actually has amazing capabilities to help us achieve any goal. It is directly connected to the source that created our being. (The same Source that Dr. Wayne Dyer talks about in his PBS show.) It becomes the servant that can fetch any dream from the universal spirit, not just find a restaurant. When the veil is dropped and truth is revealed, our potential is limitless. The current conditions of this planet are caused by too many ignorant egos.

"Without self knowledge, without understanding the working and functions of his machine, man cannot be free, he cannot govern himself and he will always remain a slave." - G. I. Gurdjieff

What's the difference between Ignorance and Apathy? - "I don't know and I don't care!" In order for us to drop the veils, we have to care. Knowledge can be acquired, but if we don't care to learn, we remain ignorant and become insignificant. New knowledge begets more caring and more caring begets the desire to learn more. If we want to change the current situation, this is the attitude we must adopt. The answer to our problems is having more of us commit to this idea.

We are all in a State of Being in the Process of Becoming. Each thought we entertain can allow us to "come to be" a higher being. This is the natural process of evolution. Growth does not happen in the conservative mind. The conservative mind is Satan personified. Virtually all advances in society were caused by liberal thinkers. The Plutarchy is concerned only with controlling the status quo, not with creating a better society. Creation and reaction contain the same letters, but only one makes sense if we are to affect change. Most people are activated by stimuli and execute actions they were taught without actually thinking. They work on the goals of the Plutarchy rather than on ones of their own choosing.

It is not positive or negative attitudes that will serve the goals. Both are necessary to define the playing field. It is Creative Mental Attitude that will destroy the veil of ego and make a better society.

Priorities

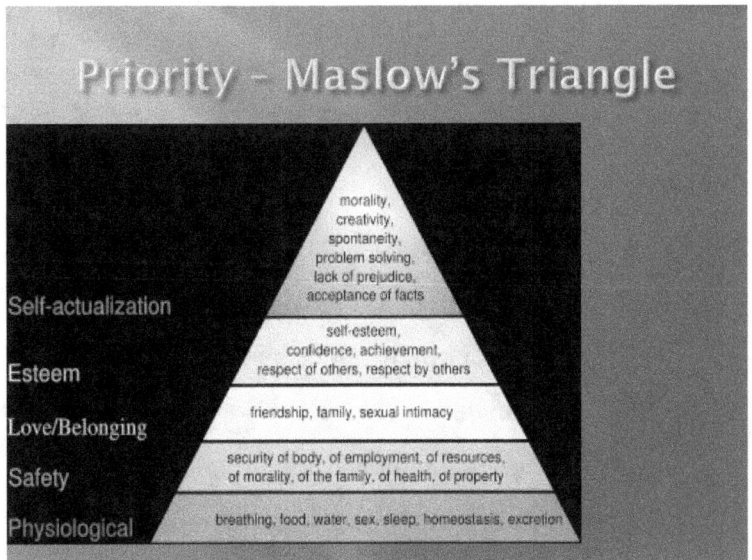

In 1949, <u>Abraham Maslow</u> published his Hierarchy of human needs. He intended to portray the motivation the ego uses to make its decisions. It classifies them by importance to the human ego.

1) Survival
2) Security
3) Social Acceptance
4) Self Esteem
5) Self Actualization

Characteristics of self-actualizers (from the website)

1) They perceive reality efficiently and tolerate uncertainty
2) Accept themselves and others for what they are
3) Spontaneous in thought and action
4) Problem-centered rather than self-centered
5) Unusual sense of humor
6) Able to look at life objectively
7) Highly creative

8) Resistant to enculturation, but not purposely unconventional
9) Concerned for the welfare of humanity
10) Capable of deep appreciation of basic life-experience
11) Establish deep interpersonal relationship with few people
12) Peak experiences
13) Need for privacy
14) Democratic attitudes
15) Strong moral and ethical standards

The above capabilities exist in all of us, but few actually activate themselves regularly and consciously to live life accordingly. Daily behaviors need to change. Behaviors leading to self-actualization:

1) Experiencing life as a child with full absorption and concentration
2) Trying new things instead of sticking to safe paths

3) Listening to feelings instead of tradition, authority or the majority
4) Avoiding pretense and being honest
5) Having no fear of being unpopular
6) Taking responsibility and doing the best possible
7) Identifying defenses and giving them up

A large percentage of the world's population never gets past social acceptance. Many will attempt and fail and their ego will shove them back into that step. Those egos run back to their various support groups to lick their wounds and perhaps give up trying. We all have a perfect being waiting inside to be discovered. Regardless of whether we tell ourselves "I can" or "I can't," we're correct. We have to know that self-esteem is created by our belief and value systems and that we judge ourselves in accordance with those elements. It is not that we weren't born perfect, only that ego is faulty in its beliefs and values. Ego's ignorance makes it stop questioning its thoughts and actions and rely on others' programming instead.

Creative Mental Attitude

We are all bipolar. The problem with having a Positive Mental Attitude is the fact that everything has to be in balance to exist. That balance point is the equal sign, so, if with have a very strong Positive Mental Attitude, the Negative Mental Attitude will be just as strong - like a magnet. If we stand in the middle of a magnet, we cannot tell which is pole is positive or negative because either side would attract with the same force. We would be in Balance. Our Peace of Mind is centered, equidistant from both ends. From that vantage point, we can examine the extent of our feelings calmly and, hopefully, creatively. This is meditation or contemplation.

Whenever we place ourselves in our center and calmly wash all thoughts from our human experience as they seek to distract us, we will feel the ends of the magnet coming closer to our true being. This can continue until the extremes of human life are removed from our minds. At that moment, we exist as the creators of whatever we can imagine. We attain the Creative Mental Attitude. This happens at the center of the two hemispheres of our brain – the Corpus Callosum.

If we can hold this point, (and we can) we then are able to restructure the thoughts in our memories in such a way that MAKES SENSE. We can do an internal sort of goals and values. This enables us to visualize our life from a different Point of View. The more we do this, the better the view becomes.

Self-Development

The development of the human form is the same as any other life on earth. An acorn contains the knowledge of becoming an oak tree, an eaglet develops into a soaring raptor, and a human baby is created by the merging of sperm cell and ovum to become what we are. All the knowledge to become whatever form is meant to be is in the DNA molecule. The double helix contains the sequence necessary to build a complete life form on one leg, along with the balance required during the process on the other leg. An influential read for me was "The Archaeology of Knowledge" by Michel Foucault:

There are many opinions formulated from the writings of Foucault. He had some interesting face offs with Noam Chomsky, for example. Chomsky is one of the great thinkers of the twentieth century and another of my influencers. What I got from Foucault's book is that the DNA molecules of my parents contained my Knowledge Base at conception. Whatever histories they had, along with their ancestors, were contained in me at the time of conception. That included the basics of how to breathe, how to eat and purge, how to exchange carbon dioxide for oxygen, etc. Each cell in my body would contain that knowledge.

As I grew and adapted to situations and experiences they had not had, my knowledge base increased and added to my parents' histories. The new knowledge was then absorbed in my cells for future generations to use. This evolution is the Process of Becoming in my mind. We are always in a State of Being in the Process of Becoming. This is true for society as well. Since society is comprised of the individuals in it, if individuals begin recognizing the knowledge they were born with and absorbing new knowledge to remove ignorance, we can change society to resemble the Lennon visualization.

In an ideal world, we would all communicate openly and honestly. If we all used de Ruiz's agreements, we could certainly be on the path to that ideal, but some egos will not want to take the time to recognize truth or will simply refuse to change their view. The ignorance/apathy cycle has to be broken for that to happen. If we don't care enough to be better, we will not seek to know better.

Self-development happens through teaching and it also happens by unlearning what is not true. There are piles of flotsam and jetsam dumped on us since birth that make it difficult to think clearly at times. We are brainwashed, domesticated, hypnotized and manipulated by the Plutarchy. We are also creatures of habit and many, if not most of us, are addicted to patterns of behavior that may be difficult to break. False beliefs and values have a huge impact on decisions. Our society is in need of debugging and that begins with debugging our own ego.

We have to stop judging ourselves and others and simply critique our results, looking for areas of improvement. To try and fail is at least to learn; to fail to try is to not know what could have been.

Experience is not the best teacher; it is the only teacher. Many people look at situations and ask why they happened to them, not knowing they were instrumental in their creation. We should imagine the future and say, "Why not?"

Thought Cycles

A thought is not a thing, it is a cycle. Our Subconscious is constantly monitoring its State of Being to find out-of-balance conditions. Any such conditions triggers thought. As George Boole describes in the "Laws of Thought," our Conscious Self (Ego) will try to identify, categorize, evaluate and decide what to do about this imbalance. That is the thought cycle. If left alone, SUBCONSCIOUS will eventually produce balance. However, Ego thinks it is smarter than SUBCONSCIOUS at times. It will make value judgments based upon its self-worth and often chooses the wrong action to regain balance. It will suffer the consequences of its foolishness.

"Nothing pains some people more that having to think"
- Dr. Martin Luther King, Jr.

- **Thought Cycles**
  - **Awareness**
  - **Attention**
  - **Analysis**
  - **Action**
  - *Adaptation*
  - *Awareness...*

All belief and value systems are imaginary and incomplete. Everything is connected to the ultimate truth and all belief is assumption. We can take as many Points of View we want, but there is only one View. Egos only argue for their points of view from a stand of ignorance. Sharing our view can improve everyone's perspective. Working together for a common goal will create a view that we can all enjoy and improve.

Time

One of the strongest programs manipulating the human mind is the calendar. In John Lennon's song, a line relates to living for today. That is a hard thing for most egos to imagine. However, it is exactly what we want to do if we wish to live according to Eckhart Tolle's "The Power of Now" in the communities of Lennon's depiction. No matter what ego believes, we always exist in the Here and Now. Here is Infinity - Now is Eternity. They comprise the balance point of our Being. It is from this point that we project what we call Reality. We broadcast our thoughts and receive the echo of their effect. That's how we create future from today.

Calendars exist to "look forward" to certain events that have not yet occurred and allow us to place mental handles on memories, future and history. We are always in NOW and project both tomorrow and yesterday into the ether to contemplate our next action. Neither truly exists. They are created in the ego mind for the purpose of making decisions. For the most part, the values of those imaginary days are created by the Plutarchy. That is how they manipulate weak minds to do things based on fantasy. We must become aware of our power to create our own reality. The best example I can think of to illustrate how to improve our ego is the movie "Groundhog Day." It is a gem to show how we can peel the ego onion.

The main character, played by Bill Murray, is a weatherman assigned to cover Punxsutawney Phil on Groundhog Day. Every year on February 2, the groundhog predicts whether or not there will be another six weeks of winter – or so the legend goes. Bill is not happy because he feels this assignment is far beneath his station in life. His ego is nasty and crusty by nature and he starts the movie obviously peeved.

He is sent there with a cameraman and a beautiful producer played by Andie McDowell. They check into their hotel the night before and go to sleep. In the morning, Bill is awakened by the radio next to the bed with: "Good morning! It's Groundhog Day! The weather for today is…." He irritably smacks the radio to end the noise and prepares for the day. He does his morning routine, gets dressed and heads for the lobby. The bellman greets him and Bill brushed him off. Along the way, he has several other chance encounters with townspeople and displays the same grumpy attitude.

When he gets to the site of the ceremony, he disgustingly watches the goings-on and gives a lackluster report on the event. Afterwards, he approaches Andie and makes a somewhat crude pass. She rebuffs him and walks away shaking her head. They pass the evening and retire to get ready for the next morning's flight home.

The next morning, Bill is awakened by the radio next to the bed with: "Good morning! It's Groundhog Day! The weather for today is…." At first, he has to collect his thoughts to see if he is dreaming and although he finds it odd, packs his suitcase and goes downstairs for breakfast. As he passes the bellman, he gets the exact same greeting as the day before. He asks what day it is and the bellman tells him its Groundhog Day. His associates are nowhere to be seen, so he ventures outside to see if they are around. No such luck, so he heads for the site of the shoot and again encounters the same people as before, saying the exact same things. His behavior the rest of the day changes ever so slightly and, puzzled, goes back to the hotel. The following morning, it's Groundhog Day again. He has no idea what is going on.

He decides to try something different. Since he knows the people he will meet from previous encounters and what they will say, he begins changing his behavior to see what new results that will bring. Because he has been repeatedly rebuffed by Andie, he tries to be nicer and brings doughnuts and coffee to her and the cameraman the next day. They are stunned and thank him for his nice gesture. He is not used to being appreciated and thanked and rather likes it. After the shoot, he again tries an awkward pass with Andie and she disappointedly refuses his advance.

The scenes depict countless Groundhog days that drive Bill bananas. He tries to break out of the day by committing suicide – jumping off buildings, stepping in front of a speeding train, etc. and still wakes up to Groundhog Day. He finally says to him, "if I'm going to be stuck in this day forever, I may as well make it as pleasant as possible." He changes his attitude. Since it appears that Andie likes him when he is nice, he will do whatever he can to get her to bed. That would be worth staying in Groundhog Day for a while.

Now, each day he rises, he pays close attention to what he says and does. He starts with the doughnuts, does a very nice report for the event and lingers after the shoot to ask Andie if she would like to have lunch with him. She is quite surprised but accepts. They have a pleasant time until his old irascible behavior returns and she leaves him behind.

The next day, he remembers where he left off with her and adjusts his manner to get through lunch successfully and they go for a walk. Again, he screws up and she angrily goes back to the hotel. Every day he gets further and further through the day until his selfish interest interferes. The movie ends when he finally is a perfect partner for her all day and they fall in love. The next morning is no longer Groundhog Day. Moral: Love is the answer.

This is how we can address our own Today. Whenever we wake up, we have a chance of improving this day by removing past ignorance from our life. In John Lennon's scenario, we can imagine living for today. Eventually, when we describe the self sustaining communities, we will describe life without calendars. That will be a challenge for most people to deal with, but it makes perfect sense if we want to reach a new paradigm.

Collective Egos

When a laboratory scientist wants to examine how an organism grows, he or she places agar into a Petri dish, adds that organism to the dish, covers it and watches its development. The organism creates a Culture. So it is with cultures among human beings. In society, agar is replaced by groups of people, the seed is a thought or idea, and the result is a School of Thought, or Ism. These schools of thought create the Cultural Ego.

Traditions, religions, institutions, political blocs and the like are examples of Cultural Egos. If an individual rebels against an ism, all kinds of punishments can be meted out by the group. Laws are written and established to maintain adherence to these artificial schools of thought and appropriate punishment is defined when violated. Moses, Confucius, Mohammed and others attempted to give guidance to the members of their society. The Ten Commandments, Shariah, etc. Cultural egos are very difficult to change. That is because the individuals within them have little idea of what they could do by thinking "outside the box."

The Plutarchy trains and domesticates its members. It is done by mutual agreement and by propagating belief and tradition that once served to unify groups. These beliefs and traditions impede the growth of thought in the individual. We have the unique ability to stop a thought and contemplate it. To behold a thought and evaluate its meaning is the most powerful capability of human beings. To pass thought back and forth through the Corpus Callosum to the emotional and intellectual hemispheres and gather meaning is a virtual miracle.

In this age of constant belaboring by the cacophony of meaningless input, it is difficult to focus on what is truly important. We have to use our ability to stop and think in order to change the path we have created. We have to prioritize our life by accepting what is important to all of us. We have to stop clicking on cultural icons to activate the apps that have been programmed into us.

If we are not willing to admit we all want the same goal, it is hopeless to discuss anything. If we do not take personal responsibility to change this world for the better, we may as well be dead already. It begins with changing our own attitude. "I'm mad as hell and I'm not going to take this anymore" is the attitude we should all adopt. Take a stand. Be willing to sacrifice everything for that stand. It is not society that creates us - it is we that create society. Be responsible, seek others who have awakened, and be a driving force for change.

We are social animals. It is important for us to belong to a group. Interaction, communication, and sharing life with others are a great part of being human. There is no need for politics in a close community. Everyone lives to contribute. Everyone feels better after doing a good deed for someone else. There is no reason why this concept cannot go global. What we choose to do with this idea is up to each of us. If we do not come together to further our species in a common sense manner, we cannot change the current situation.

The current situation includes the doubling of the human population in the last fifty years or so. It includes the pollution of most, if not all, fresh water. It includes the pollution of the air we breathe to the point that chronic asthma and bronchitis flourish. It includes global warming, proliferation of weapons, drugs, crime, power and greed. How long we remain spectators instead of participants is yet to be known. We must be insane. We are like Nero fiddling while Rome burns.

Mind Control should belong to each of us, and it does. We simply have to know when we are thinking for ourselves and when we are activating ourselves with someone else's programming. Before opening our minds to any idea or experience that is strange and new, it has to pass a test before we spend any of our time and attention on it. Too many of us will have a knee-jerk reaction to stimuli we receive and categorically reject trying to understand something because we have a preconceived notion of it. To open our mind to possibilities, we have to question that reaction.

1) Why am I reacting this way?
2) What does this stimulus REALLY mean to me?
3) What is it connected to?
4) Why does it exist in my mind?
5) Is it true?
6) How can knowledge of it help me?

When we contemplate something in this manner, we have become AWARE of its reality in our own mind. We can stay as long as we want in this State of Being, contemplating anything we choose. This is what Gautama Siddartha did under the Bodhi tree (for three years) before starting his teaching. He achieved number 3 above when he realized everything in the Universe is connected. He discovered Truth within himself and eventually achieved Nirvana to become the first Buddha.

Truth and Trust have four letters in common. If we cannot or will not trust ourselves to understand, there will be no changing of mind. We will stay trapped in our own web of ignorance. We must know that we all have the same abilities developed to different levels. For any endeavor, there are tyros, apprentices, journeymen and masters. So it is with individual minds. Truth resides in all of us and we should try to uncover it.

"Everyone is born a genius, but the process of living de-geniuses them."
— Richard Buckminster Fuller

To discover Truth in ourselves, we must also trust the source of the communication we receive. If we relinquish our trusting capability to those who just want to control us, we will not develop past ignorance and will remain under their influence. We can avoid this by knowing that we all contain the Truth from birth and do not need any help from "outside" to find it. We just need to ask ourselves if something can be true. We know. The human ego is the only entity on earth that can lie and accept lies as truth.

When faced with a decision about the thoughts we contemplate, we have the reaction called "Fight or Flight." We either face it or try to avoid it. It's not difficult to know what to do when we smell smoke in the house or the ladder is teetering beneath us, but, when we speak of matters of the mind, it becomes more difficult to make the correct choice. That choice should be to face the thought and fight to understand it. That occurs when we Pay Attention and hold the thought in mind while seeking connections to that thought. Intelligence tries to connect thoughts while ignorant ego seeks to judge and separate. Today's environment bombards minds with so many thoughts that it is difficult to hold an attention span for very long. We need to think in peace and focus on understanding to develop our lives.

Thoughts we choose to contemplate are numerous and they are prioritized by our ego's Value System.

The goals we choose to achieve something are assigned a value by the ego for the purpose of increasing its self-worth. We are always working on our Number One Goal in the Here and Now. If self-knowledge and understanding are not near the top of the ego's Wish List, not much progress will be made. Ego will make excuses to remain ignorant – "I'm too busy; I already have enough knowledge; this is too hard; it's malarkey, etc," rather than make a sincere effort to find Truth. Maintaining focus is hard in this state because Truth will bring down any ego to equality with everyone and everything else.

Ego is the only thing that can slow down the creation of Lennon's ideal society. It lives in a "Comfort Zone" of its own making and does not like to be disturbed. Sometimes, it takes disasters to rouse it from its nest. These disasters can be natural, like climate change, hurricanes and volcanoes, or political, like destroying the twin towers in New York to create wars. Wars exist because of sick egos and mind control by the Plutarchy.

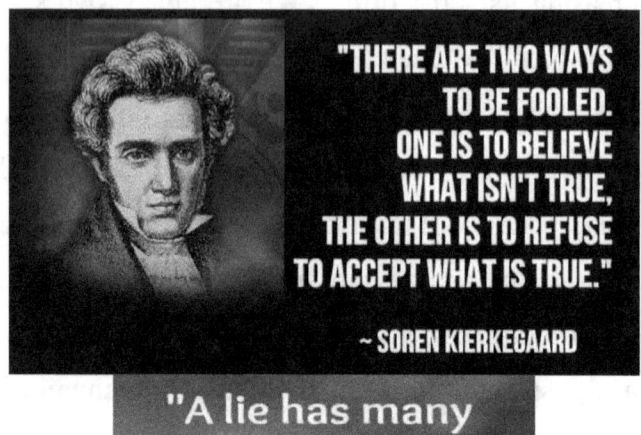

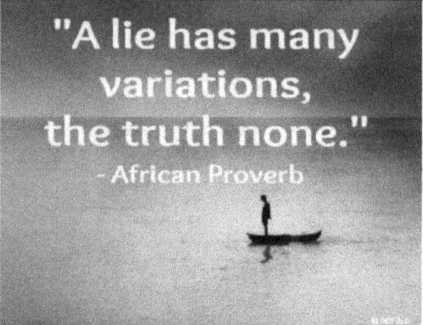

Only Truth can set all of us free. We must communicate it to each other at all times to tame the ego forever.

The Johari Window

On February 5, 1982, I experienced an epiphany. It has occurred several times since then. There is no doubt in my mind that we can all experience it. Call it Rapture. The experience was caused by a training class I attended in California called "Counselor Selling," from Wilson Learning Corporation.

"Counselor Selling" is a five-day course in professional sales. Larry Wilson, founder of Wilson Learning, created the class. It is, in my mind, the best sales course for pros. The elements that changed my life were the description of the Sales Cycle and the Johari Window. The Sales Cycle has four steps: Establish Trust, Establish Need, Establish Fit, and Establish Hurry. I didn't like the word hurry, so I refer to that step as Establish Timing.

After the course ended, I began thinking about this cycle and applying it to all the decisions I had made in the past. It was a monumental purge of my historical mistakes. I extended the thoughts to other elements of my life and suddenly realized how this thing called "life" is totally interconnected. That weekend was spent driving up and down the California coast in tears. Ecstasy! This experience was my turning point. It is best described in the introduction to "Transforming the Mind," available for free on the Internet:

"You may, at some time, have had a 'peak' experience, an ecstatic moment or a moment of greater understanding, when your consciousness expanded - and you knew it. When this occurs, the integration between left brain (logical thinking) and right brain (intuitive feelings and emotions) is manifested in increased energy-flow between the two sides. This is thinking and feeling in a holistic and balanced way. It is a foretaste of an evolutionary jump for humanity - and in essence, what the so-called New Age is all about - a new level of maturity in mental development, an awakening.

By learning how to arouse the whole brain, selectively and at will, the mode of consciousness may be freely altered, appropriate to the task or situation - whether a crisis, making music, relaxing, mental arithmetic, brainstorming, or contemplating nature. In this new wide-awake consciousness, the world seems to be full of possibilities – it possesses a strong sense of rediscovered meaning. This is nothing mystical. It is essentially ordinary consciousness, operating for once at its proper efficiency."

This is also what Dr. Jill-Bolte Taylor writes about in her "Stroke of Insight."

There was no going back. One of the segments in Counselor Selling is the discussion of the Johari Window. This added impact to my new understanding. For the class, it was depicted as a quadrant and supposedly defined human characteristics when communicating with one another. This was the reason for my contacting Larry Wilson when I returned from Saudi Arabia and resulted in his invitation to me to come to his Pecos River Learning Center.

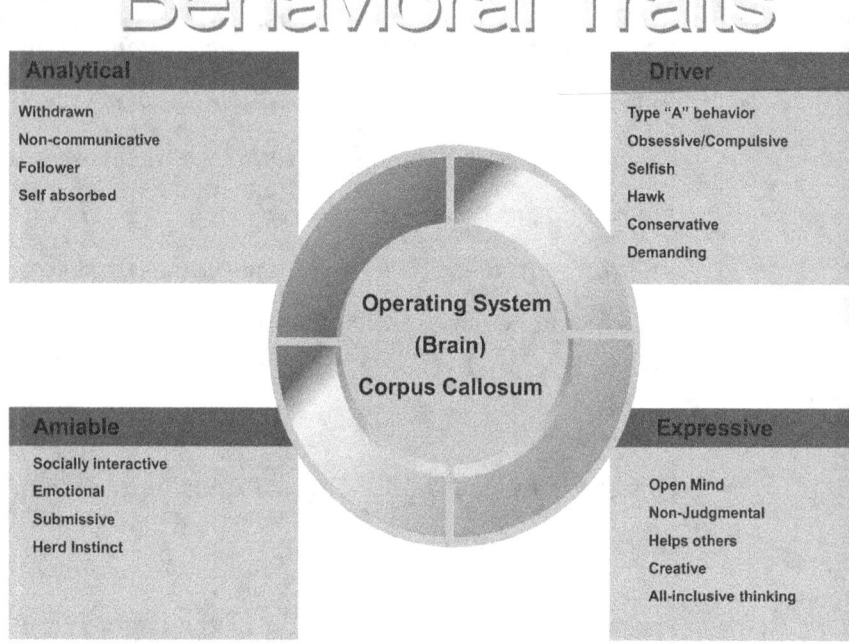

Behavioral Traits

Analytical
Withdrawn
Non-communicative
Follower
Self absorbed

Driver
Type "A" behavior
Obsessive/Compulsive
Selfish
Hawk
Conservative
Demanding

Operating System
(Brain)
Corpus Callosum

Amiable
Socially interactive
Emotional
Submissive
Herd Instinct

Expressive
Open Mind
Non-Judgmental
Helps others
Creative
All-inclusive thinking

This is my interpretation of the Johari Window

The Johari Window classifies the different personality traits people use to communicate to others. For the class, it was depicted as a two-dimensional window segmented into four quadrants: Analytical, Amiable, Driver and Expressive.

If we were to imagine the center vertical line as average Intelligence Quotient (IQ) and the center horizontal line as average Emotional Quotient (EQ), we find that the Expressive block is the only one that contains individuals with higher-than-average of both IQ and EQ. These are the Self-Actualized leaders we want. Their types are identified in books like "Good to Great" and "In Search of Excellence." The four blocks are also defined by an Asian saying:

He who knows not and knows not that he knows not (Analytical) is a fool; shun him.

He who knows not and knows he knows not (Driver) is a student; teach him.

He who knows and knows not that he knows (Amiable) is asleep; wake him.

He who knows and knows that he knows (Expressive) is wise; follow him.

A couple of years before I attended this class, I attended another great sales training session in Atlanta. The course leader pointed out similar traits, but described them in a three-dimensional model, rather than a two-dimensional window. Upon further thinking, I imagined our personality as a sphere, rotating as Mother Earth does. When encountering another sphere, we make contact and based on each other's attitude and adjust to begin conversation on Common Ground. The more we share, the more we bond and bring the spheres further into agreement with each other. That bond defines the strength of any relationship.

Many Analyticals who begin reading this book will fall by the wayside because they "don't know – don't care." (I shorten their category name to Anals.) The Anals are ultra-conservatives who hang on to untrue and/or outdated concepts. They will eventually disappear through attrition and education but the unfortunate part is that they can vote. The problem is whether or not we can save the planet before they are gone or educated.

Lastly, there are small spheres and large spheres that represent the scope of understanding each person contains. That defines the size of the sphere, jar, box or envelope each person lives in. The sphere we control is our Sphere of Influence. Larry Wilson was very happy with this description when I presented it to him at his ranch. That's when he called all his employees to listen to what I was saying. Those that create problems for the planet are small minds, or spheres, and those who have gone insane with power – like the Fascist Plutarchy.

If we are to look at the total population of the world and hope to salvage Mother Earth, we must inject truth into this model so that more people can see their potential. We will always have IQ and EQ averages at 100, but we can raise awareness in the population to make those averages become much more than what they mean today. That is done by education. People who do not want to learn may not be of much help, but they will have no choice but to follow. We cannot wait for them to understand.

Conservatives reside in the Analytical and Driver blocks. They have not yet crossed the horizontal line into caring about others. The Fascist Plutarchy lives in the Driver block and maintains power through the use of money and ignorance. It rewards its followers with special privileges to continue their support. If one of their cronies in another country does not toe the line, he is deposed by creating social unrest or military bullying. This is the primary reason for worldwide unification.

If we adopt the Five Agreements as our Code of Conduct for communicating with each other and we share our experiences and views, there is nothing that can stop us from creating a dream that befits all. John Lennon's "Imagine" befits any Expressive.

Equality for all is an ideal contained in many science fiction novels. Star Trek is a good example of a future society. If you've seen any episodes that include revisiting Earth, you know that we have evolved into a society as described by Lennon's song in those episodes. There is no want, no greed, and no money to distinguish one world citizen from another. People still enjoy expressing their purpose, but are not programmed to do unnatural acts, like killing others. The key to this scenario is the use of technology to serve, rather than control the population. We are at a point to make this happen.

The difference between that society and the one we are currently living in is simple. In the future, everyone has access to the whole body of knowledge gathered to date. There are no secrets to create doubt and fear in people's minds. There is no money to create crime, no politicians to grasp power and no borders to restrict movement about the planet. There is enough to feed, clothe and shelter everyone, so everyone shares equally. People are free to express their inner purpose and do not compare or judge actions and results outside of their own being.

Creating as a group is now much more powerful and efficient than creating alone. If we wish to create interstellar vehicles as a society, let's do it! If we can think it, it must be possible. We do not yet know how, but there is an unlimited fountain of knowledge that can be accessed for discovering ways to create what we imagine. We will either survive or perish as a group. Creating the future as a group is much more appealing than arguing about methods of control.

Politics

Today's world is being destroyed due to politics.

Pros and Cons

A debate is communication about a topic from two opposing Points of View. At the highest levels of debates, ideas and ideals are the standard topics. If we are to create John Lennon's vision, we have to lift our minds to the intangible part of our minds. The objective of debate is not just to present our Point of View and stop; it is also to reach a common agreement of what the topic really means. It usually is aimed at making progress towards achieving a goal or reaching higher standards.

Progress implies an advance of society over time toward a better state of civilization by movement forward into time. Congress can be defined as a formal meeting of delegates to discuss matters of concern or mutual interest. "Gress" means to walk or, loosely, to take action. We appear to be at a standstill when it comes to decision-making in

Congress. Progress is stalled. Debate has turned into a popularity matchup pitting progress against greed and power. The rights and welfare of citizens being governed are far down the agenda.

The "cons" in this scenario is short for conservatives. They are the selfish, greedy, and heartless egos that will resist change to prevent progress. Cons are also defined as criminals (convicts) and this definition surely befits conservatives. They represent the satanic side of the debate. They will fight very hard to prevent Lennon's song from materializing. The Plutarchy that leads this group must be overcome to make progress toward a peaceful society.

Our mass media are used universally by the Plutarchy to communicate messages that serve to prevent protest, rather than communicate truth.

> *"When I was born, humanity was 95 per cent illiterate. Since I've been born, the population has doubled and that total population is now 65 per cent literate. That's a gain of 130-fold of the literacy. When humanity is primarily*

illiterate, it needs leaders to understand and get the information and deal with it. When we are at the point where the majority of humans them-selves are literate, able to get the information, we're in an entirely new relationship to Universe. We are at the point where the integrity of the individual counts and not what the political leadership or the religious leadership says to do."
— Richard Buckminster Fuller, *Only Integrity Is Going to Count: Integrity Day, Los Angeles February 26, 1983*

The Plutarchy rules by hiding truth from the population. They use communication media like television, radio, newspapers to distract, deflect and manipulate minds that cannot or will not think for themselves. Propaganda, indoctrination, false values and beliefs are disseminated through these channels and polls are taken to gauge their effect.

They are in conflict with PBS, National Public Radio, Greenpeace, Sierra Club, Save the Earth foundation and other such organizations attempting to present the facts. The chink in their armor happens to be social media on the Internet. Witness the events in Egypt, Libya, Syria and other protests against this ruling class. Even if we do not get actively involved in the above groups, we should support their efforts.

I categorize the Plutarchy running this world into three possibilities:

1) Aliens from another planet
2) Illuminati gone wild
3) Insanity

4) Overpopulation

I find it difficult to think that any advanced civilization capable of interstellar travel would be as cruel as we are. After studying "Mastery of Life" from the Rosicrucians, I think their ideals are reasonable. I was turned off after three years because of rituals I considered antiquated. The third option is more probable. Power has a way of making people crazy. It is relatively simple to wrest power from the Plutarchy, though. We just need enough people to unite.

It is even more probable that the time has come to cull the herds. The population bubble is much more significant than the real estate crash. If Monsanto is indeed using Genetically Modified Organisms (GMOs) to poison the food supply, this is already underway. If pharmaceuticals are adding substances to their myriad of (cures) to support this effort, we can understand the reasoning, but, is that the only way to restore balance on earth?

This past presidential election was a great example of power gone mad. Untold billions wasted on trying to fool naïve Americans into electing another idiot. That money could have done some good for the world. Conservative thinking is what is killing this planet - selfish, greedy, heartless, ignorant conservative thinking. The Plutarchy lost this one because enough people woke up. Even more will wake up before the next election. It may be interesting to note that greed and corruption are especially prevalent in four very well-known countries – The United States, Australia, Canada and Great Britain. These governments are trying to muffle protests, take individual weapons away, and cooperating with Corporate Oil to a much higher degree than others. "The sun never sets on the British Empire" comes to mind from olden days.

Dear Friends in the USA,
Don't vote Romney.

Regards,
The Rest of the World.

History is a lie
Religion is a control system
Money is a hoax
Debt is a fiction
Media is manipulation
Government is a corporation
The system is a lie

Wake Up

Anarchy doesn't mean chaos or disorder, it means freedom from an oppressive centralised authority with a monopoly on force.

It is horrifying that we have to fight our own government to save the environment.
— Ansel Adams —

When I was in California some years ago, the company that hired me had a cocktail party to celebrate the end of a training session and one of the executives came to me and asked where I lived:

"Chicago," I replied.

"Ah, a concrete head, eh!" he said.

"What's that?" I asked.

"That's someone whose mind is all mixed up and permanently set!" That is a conservative.

It's time to rid ourselves of tyrants, satraps and dictators. It's time to unite and create a better world. We need an Occupy Earth movement to merge all of us into one voice. Greenpeace, Sierra Club and other organizations can blend their members into the mix. We need to start draining power from the Plutarchy with unified protests, boycotts and civil disobedience in a non-violent show of force. Millions and millions are ready to join. Earth Day should be celebrated on the first Monday of every month instead of once a year. No driving, no shopping, no television or radio. Stay home with family and friends and start a green project every month.

The Plutarchy is made up of the military/industrial complex, the banking system, insurance companies, pharmaceuticals, chemical giants and corporations. It seems like a daunting task to bring them down from their ivory towers, but it must be done. More and more of them are identifying themselves and we have to remove their power as soon as possible.

When I was selling software to the Fortune 500, I sent for all their Annual reports. There, I found that most of their networks are linked through the Board of Directors. They make sure they maintain their power by supporting each others' financial needs and set the stage for the next Annual Report to be more profitable. Imagine them rubbing their hands together in glee when they found out the Bush administration decided to start a war. Many of the corporations veil their intent by producing parts of a greater whole in secret and secured smaller companies.

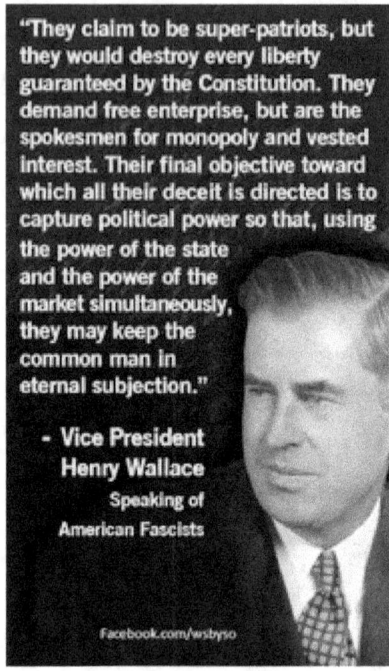

"They claim to be super-patriots, but they would destroy every liberty guaranteed by the Constitution. They demand free enterprise, but are the spokesmen for monopoly and vested interest. Their final objective toward which all their deceit is directed is to capture political power so that, using the power of the state and the power of the market simultaneously, they may keep the common man in eternal subjection."

- Vice President Henry Wallace
Speaking of American Fascists

Facebook.com/wsbyso

Fascism: any movement, ideology, or attitude that favors dictatorial government, centralized control of private enterprise, repression of all opposition, and extreme nationalism. That is the definition of today's Republican Party. Abraham Lincoln, Teddy Roosevelt and Dwight D. Eisenhower would have these people on trial for trying to represent our Republic.

If you like the panels above, you can find more here.

Religion

1. **beliefs and worship:** people's beliefs and opinions concerning the existence, nature, and worship of a deity or deities, and divine involvement in the universe and human life

2. **system:** an institutionalized or personal system of beliefs and practices relating to the divine

3. **personal beliefs or values:** a set of strongly-held beliefs, values, and attitudes that somebody lives by

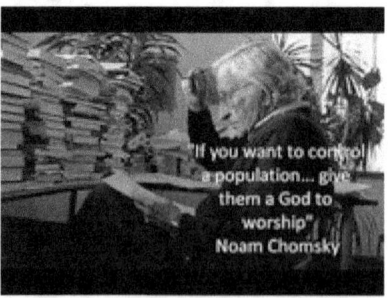

Organized religion uses the need for socialization to indoctrinate its believers. We all want to be part of a group of like minds that we can agree

with and enjoy the company. That's why we create clubs, organizations and gangs. We are at a juncture in history that creates a confrontation between logic and belief. A belief is only an assumption supported by faith. Science questions its findings continually to try and disprove what it has discovered. Religion doesn't want its believers to question doctrine. There is much inspiration in the Bible, Torah and Koran that strikes a resounding chord in the reader, but much of what is written is pure fantasy and fiction.

With the materials of the day, Noah's ark would never even have floated, yet we have individuals scouring mountains in Turkey for its remains. How ignorant is this? How would Noah have gathered kangaroos and Tasmanian devils – FedEx or DHL? How could the earth be covered in water that receded for landfall? Has anyone heard of the water table?

When I lived in Saudi Arabia, there were not many distractions or amusements available. No bars, no movies, no amusement parks, no sports arenas, no tourist attractions and no radio or television other than Koran lessons. Since I worked for a Saudi company and associated with primarily Saudi clients, I was invited to private homes often. There were basically two topics of conversation during my visits – politics and religion.

Thirteen centuries before Jesus, stories were written of virgin birth and other legends and they carried through the Bible and Koran. Five hundred years before Jesus, the first Buddha spread the word of kindness, beauty and harmony with nature and neighbors for over forty years. If we want to believe in miracles, let's believe in the fact that we are conscious of our Universe. That's miracle enough. Let's not let the Plutarchy poison our children's minds any more. They will have to solve the problems we caused them. Fantasy won't work.

I was always asked about my religion in Saudi Arabia. I had been raised as a Catholic and was familiar with the Bible and Koran. When I filled in the form to apply for entry into the country, I wrote "Christian" in the religion block. I am convinced that Jesus existed and was crucified and I am convinced that there is a power that holds this universe together, but I do not believe there is any sin other than wanting to stay ignorant. Discussing politics and religion on a regular basis with Saudis who held masters degrees and doctorates from Western institutions was quite pleasant and educational. Most of these educated hosts had risen above organized religion and it was common for wives to be sporting jeans and tee shirts inside the home. I was honored to be trusted in their casual environment.

Religion is about belief and faith. These elements create assumptions. De Ruiz' third agreement is to avoid assumptions. The problem with discussing religion is that we eventually have to admit WHY we believe what we believe. The answer should not be "because the Bible tells me so." The answer is a deep-rooted desire of wanting to know "Why am I alive?" Today's evangelical fundamentalists are not Christians for the simple reason they believe in the book, not the message Jesus was trying to convey. Their ranting and raving and creating apologetics to explain their ignorance is anti-Christ. Anyone who tries to convince another that the earth and Universe is around six thousand years old is a blooming idiot. Anyone who is willing to believe it is a concrete-headed moron.

We all need some firmament to hold onto as we wend our way through life, but fantasy is not going to help. Only truth can set us free. Organized religions are prisons that shackle the minds of the believers. They indoctrinate by repetition, rituals, and group agreement to the point that one's ego would be worthless by letting go of false beliefs and values. That's what we need to do – let go the ego. In the definitions above, all contain the word "belief." Belief is not knowledge. A belief is an opinion, an assumption, or both. Doctrine is a school of thought that activates certain behaviors in individuals based upon the circumstances. It resembles "apps" that we download into our electronic gadgets. Religion can be a very addicting habit.

Sometimes I wonder if people simply don't want to know the truth because it would make their belief and value systems obsolete.

Non-religion

"Buddhism has the characteristics of what would be expected in a cosmic religion for the future: It transcends a personal god, avoids dogmas and theology; it covers both the natural and spiritual; and it is based on a religious sense aspiring from the experience of all things, natural and spiritual, as a meaningful unity." — Albert Einstein

I disagree with Einstein's quote a little bit. To me, religion makes use of belief systems, whereas Buddhism does not. If anything, I would call it a non-religion. It is a method of peeling the ego's layers of false beliefs and assumptions. Five hundred years before Jesus, Gauthama Siddartha, the first Buddha, described the ultimate goal for us to be attaining Nirvana which is reached through enlightenment. He spent forty-five years teaching others to help them reach the same realization. When he died, he passed through pari nirvana, which means completed nirvana.

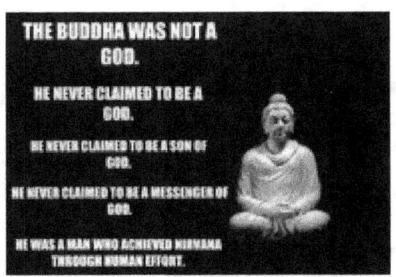

THE BUDDHA WAS NOT A GOD.

HE NEVER CLAIMED TO BE A GOD.

HE NEVER CLAIMED TO BE A SON OF GOD.

HE NEVER CLAIMED TO BE A MESSENGER OF GOD.

HE WAS A MAN WHO ACHIEVED NIRVANA THROUGH HUMAN EFFORT.

"Some people, when we talk about compassion and love, think it is a religious matter. Compassion is the universal religion." – Dalai Lama

Nirvana is the most misunderstood term in Buddhism. Some in the West recognize the term as meaning Heaven, or a Heaven on Earth, or perhaps a famous rock band.

Nirvana literally means extinguishing or unbinding. The implication is that it is freedom from what ever binds you, from the burning passion of desire, jealousy, and ignorance. Once these are totally overcome, a state of bliss is achieved, and there is no longer the need for the cycle of birth and death. All karmic debts are settled. I call it taming the ego.

The Buddha saw Nirvana as a much different state than our current existence, and not a simple parallel to the process of individual rebirth. In Buddhist philosophy, this is becoming an arhat, a person who has reached the highest level of enlightenment without yet becoming a Buddha.

An Arhat literally translates as worthy of offerings, without birth, and killer of thieves. An eminent monk or saint who has achieved a level of enlightenment, but is not yet a Buddha. An Arhat or Lohan is one who has overcome outward manifestation of afflicting emotions, but who has not completely eliminated their psychic imprint. Although free of the cycle of birth and death, an Arhat is not fully enlightened. These holy beings are also called Venerable Ones or foe-destroyers. This is the first stage of liberation or ending the cycle of birth and death and goal of the Hinayana sects. The Arhat is said to be beyond both merit and demerit because, as he has abandoned all defilements, he can no longer perform evil actions;

and as he has no more attachment, his virtuous actions no longer bear karmic fruit.

Progress on the path of an Arhat is measured by the person's ability to weaken or eliminate the ten fetters which bind him to the cycle of birth and death, and which keep him from attaining Nirvana. There are four recognizable stages which mark his progress along the path. These are explained in relation to the ten fetters below.

At the first stage is the Stream-winner or Stream-enterer (srotapanna), that is, one who has entered the "stream" that eventually leads to the "Ocean of Nirvana." When he is at this stage, his insight is powerful enough to remove the first three fetters, namely:

> (1) the belief in the existence of permanent self;
> (2) doubt in the ability of the Three Gems to lead him towards the goals

> (3) The mistaken belief that moral rules and ascetic rites alone are sufficient to lead a person to Enlightenment.

On attaining this first stage, the would-be Arhat will no longer be reborn in any of the lower realms of existence. He will be reborn no more than seven times in the human or heavenly planes of existence before he attains Nirvana.

As he makes further progress and perfects his insight still more, he reaches the second stage of the Once-Returner (sakrdagamin). After this life, he will be reborn only once more as a human being. In that rebirth, he would attain Nirvana. At this stage, he has also succeeded in weakening the fourth and fifth fetters. These are critical for the arhat to continue progress toward Nirvana,

> 4)   attachment to sensual desire, creature

comforts and selfish interests; and
(5)   ill will.

The third stage is that of the Non-Returner or no-more-rebirths (anagamin). At this stage, he completely removes the fourth and fifth fetters of attachment to sensual desire and ill will. The Non-Returner will no longer be reborn in the human realm; he will be reborn in one of the Pure Abodes in the heavens where he will attain Nirvana. At this stage, the first five fetters have been totally removed.

At the fourth stage, he makes the final advance towards becoming an arhat or Foe-destroyer who attains nirvana because he has broken all the ten fetters, the last five of which are:

(6)   Desire for existence in the worlds of Form; but rather in the true Spirit of Living

(7)   Desire for existence in the Formless Worlds of Consciousness, Eternity and Infinity;

(8)   Refuting forever the attraction of conceit, selfishness and Ego construction;

(9)   Restlessness;

(10)   Ignorance.

The career of the Arhat is like the career of a student in that development is measured by the highest stage or level he has achieved so far. When a secondary school student progress in stages from that of a Freshman to that of a Senior, his knowledge and mastery of skill increase with each higher level achieved. Eventually, he graduates from school when he passes his final year examinations. In the same way, the would-be Arhat overcomes more and more of the fetters at each higher stage of his development. When he successfully passes the fourth stage, he reaches the end of his career and is no longer subject to rebirth. However, he is not yet at the highest stage. He is not yet a Buddha.

One who is on any of the first three stages on this path is called a "sekha," or a Striver-on-the-Path.

One of the books that got me interested in this line of thinking is "Time, Space, and Knowledge," by Tarthang Tulku. Commonly referred to as TSK, there are many websites available to gain more knowledge about this book. He further divides these terms into Ordinary TSK and Great TSK. The book contains about three dozen exercises for the seeker to perform to help break free of ego's grasp and proceed on the Tao. I interpret the Ordinary as the physical human life and the Great as the divine spiritual life.

Because Buddhism does not recognize sin and rebuffs the ego's demands, it clears the seeker's mind of guilt. We are all doing the best we can under the circumstances in our view of Time, Space, and Knowledge and, we follow the Tao to enlightenment; we improve along the way.

"Your enlightenment rests on your own shoulders."
– Dalai Lama

Regardless of one's view of Buddhism, it is important to point out that kindness, compassion, joyfulness, affection, brotherhood, peace and similar words are continually used in describing the way to live. I don't know if Yoko Ono influenced John Lennon to write the words to "Imagine," but I would have no trouble believing it. The words resound with Buddhist attitudes.

"Change takes place through action. Not through prayer or meditation, but through action." – Dalai Lama

About ten years after familiarizing myself with Buddhism, I read "The Four Agreements" by de Ruiz. In it, he describes the Toltec Nagal as a Spiritual Warrior. Toltecs were scientific spiritualists with understanding of life similar to Buddha. There is a huge movement underway to spread the word about this on the Internet. The four agreements follow the same kind of thoughts as Buddhist teachings.

The last non-religion I looked into is Metaphysics. To me, this is the Grand Unification Theory (GUT) that so many physicists are trying to prove with higher mathematics – from the microcosm through the macrocosm is one unified whole.

At the top of Maslow's Hierarchy of Needs is Transcendence. It is the underlying goal for all of us (according to Maslow) and is purely spiritual. It is attained by recognizing truth and nothing but the truth. We can call it Nirvana, as well. At the top of the pyramid on the Great Seal of the United States is the Eye of Horus, overlooking the world from its transcendent perch.

The Dalai Lama is in New York for the first time and is told about the delicious hot dogs sold by street vendors. He is taken to a nearby stand:

> "What's your pleasure, Mac?" asks the vendor.

> "One – with everything."

"It appears to me (whether rightly or wrongly) that direct arguments against Christianity and theism produce hardly any effect on the public; and freedom of thought is best promoted by the gradual illumination of men's minds which follows from the advance of science." [Charles Darwin]

"If we believe absurdities, we shall commit atrocities." [Voltaire]

"I cannot imagine a God who rewards and punishes the objects of his creation, whose purposes are modeled after our own -- a God, in short, who is but a reflection of human frailty. Neither can I believe that the individual survives the death of his body, although feeble souls harbor such thoughts through fear or ridiculous egotism." [Albert Einstein]

"Faith means not wanting to know what is true." [Nietzsche]

"I cannot believe in the immortality of the soul.... No, all this talk of an existence for us, as individuals, beyond the grave is wrong. It is born of

*our tenacity of life – our desire to go on living ...
our dread of coming to an end.* " [Thomas Edison]

*"The Bible is not my book nor Christianity my
profession. I could never give assent to the long,
complicated statements of Christian dogma.*"
[Abraham Lincoln]

*"Religion is a byproduct of fear. For much of
human history, it may have been a necessary evil,
but why was it more evil than necessary? Isn't
killing people in the name of God a pretty good
definition of insanity?*" [Arthur C. Clarke]

*"Religions are all alike – founded upon fables and
mythologies.* " [Thomas Jefferson]

*"Say what you will about the sweet miracle of
unquestioning faith, I consider a capacity for it
terrifying and absolutely vile.*" [Kurt Vonnegut]

*"Religion is based . . . mainly on fear . . . fear of the
mysterious, fear of defeat, fear of death. Fear is the
parent of cruelty, and therefore it is no wonder if*

cruelty and religion have gone hand in hand. . . .
My own view on religion is that of Lucretius. I
regard it as a disease born of fear and as a source
of untold misery to the human race." [Bertrand
Russell]

Spirituality is where truth resides. Indoctrination
should stop.

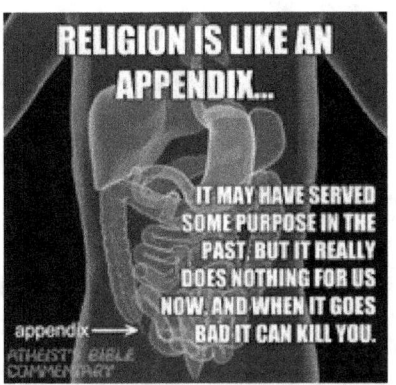

RELIGION IS LIKE AN APPENDIX...

IT MAY HAVE SERVED SOME PURPOSE IN THE PAST, BUT IT REALLY DOES NOTHING FOR US NOW, AND WHEN IT GOES BAD IT CAN KILL YOU.

appendix →

ATHEIST BIBLE COMMENTARY

When Descartes coined his famous "Cogito, ergo sum," it was supposedly to prove the existence of a god. It is impossible to disagree that there is something to this consciousness we call Life. All languages that I know have a verb that means "to be." In my native French, the term "raison d'être" means "reason for being." Everything that manifests in our consciousness has a reason for being. Descartes tried to explain this with logic and connect that logic with a Supreme Being.

Bucky Fuller said "God is supreme Being, the verb, not the noun." He understood that it is not what we name something that carries value for us, but what it does. Our Subconscious values manifestations for what they do, not what we call them as human beings. It knows their reason for being. If we ask ourselves what the reason for our being may be, we may find the peace of mind we all seek.

I know God exists, but I do not visualize Supreme Being as some anthropomorphized entity with human characteristics. All of us know that there must be more to living than mindlessly performing mundane tasks. If we are to know God, we cannot separate ourselves from Him. Our consciousness is created IN his image, not in His IMAGE. All consciousness of every being in created IN His image. Jesus said: *"Look inside; the Kingdom of God is within you."*

If we know that our Intelligent Design is the same for all creation, we must admit that our planet is part of this design. Bucky Fuller proposed that the earth is an organism just as we are, and named Mother Earth "Gaea," (also spelled "Gaia.") Part of the reason this rings true is that every atom comprising our bodies came from Gaea as well as all other life treading on her face. We are dust and into dust, we shall return.

We probably all know that the Equator separates the planet from North and South. If Bucky Fuller is right that Gaea is an organism, just as we are, then she must have the same characteristics as we do. She must have frequency and amplitude capabilities, like the two hemispheres we have in our brain and use the universal "Common Sense" to feel her environment. Her efforts to keep herself in homeostasis by sensing that environment and executing a sequence of steps to regain balance would mirror our own efforts when we react to a feeling of imbalance. The only difference would be that she has no ego.

When I lived in Saudi Arabia and mingled with others from various parts of the globe, I took notice of the way people communicate with their native language. It is a fact that some cultures use language and the writing of that language differently. Arabic is written and read from right to left, so is Hebrew, so is Chinese, Japanese, etc. Western languages are written and read from left to right.

Additionally, written Eastern languages do not use letters as the Western languages do. Chinese, Japanese and others use actual pictograms to convey messages. Western languages use alphabets to create words, sentences and paragraphs to convey meaning during communication. The interesting aspect of these observations is that the line of demarcation for these differences is perpendicular to the Equator through the Middle East. In fact, if we were to draw a line from the North Pole to the South Pole through Mecca, it would approximate that demarcation. In the area near that line, we find combinations of both methods of communication like the Kabbalah, which uses both letters and symbols united to convey meaning.

Gaea's left hemisphere appears to mirror ours, the digital side to the West and her right hemisphere seems to mirror our analog side to the East. They make up Thought and Feeling (Common Sense.) As her creatures, she would endow us with those same facilities, as well as all her other creatures. The only logical conclusion is that our bodies are indeed made in the image of our creator – Gaea.

Gaea is also one of God's creations and therefore, as perfect as our TRUE selves. I would never, ever consider killing my mother, but that is what humanity is doing. Anyone who approaches me professing a faith in whatever "god" is in his or her mind and then throws trash on the sidewalk is immediately pegged as a hypocrite or ignoramus.

The Universe that IS God was supposedly set in motion by the Word, "Let there be Light!" Not the bedroom lamp, but the Light of Consciousness. That's all God had to do for that Universe to evolve to today. Only two laws need be known in that universe – Law of Balance and Law of Sequence. The double helix of our DNA exemplifies these laws perfectly. Evolution happens when a being has to adapt to changing conditions in its environment. We must obey Gaea's Balance of Nature or perish by her reaction. We must stop worshipping some imaginary Santa Claus in the sky and get serious. The human ego is the only Satan and he surely exists in those who believe he is real. Satan is created the same way as Santa, the same letters are reorganized, and that's all.

Could it be possible that every ailment we suffer could be a reflection of the ailments we impose upon our mother?

Could it be that the destruction of her immune system (ozone layer) is why she gave us AIDS?

Could it be that our cities (cancers on her skin) causes cancers in us?

Could it be that giving her a fever (global warming) is causing fits and shivers shown by unusual and unprecedented climate events?

When will we wakeup? Why do we continue on the path to suicide?

(1) Destroying the life-giving rain forest that developed for providing us with oxygen and is the source of natural remedies;

(2) Scraping the bottom of oceans by commercial fisherman and destroying habitat for untold species;

(3) Creating a dump in the middle of the Pacific as large as Texas that can actually be seen by satellites;

(4) Building pipelines through her natural beauty like cat scratches on our face;

(5) Polluting our ground water with techniques like fracking; and many other atrocities we commit means doom to us, not to her.

We can hold to our image of God, but we first must understand where our bodies came from. Our spirit comes from the totality of God, but our bodies belong to Gaea.

The Earth does not belong to us...

We belong to the Earth.
–Chief Seattle
Suquamish and Duwamish

Join Greenpeace, Sierra Club, Save the Earth Foundation or any other of the myriad organizations fighting the insanity of our societal leaders. You'll be happy to be involved in healing our dear mother. Our "raison d'être" is surely not to commit suicide.

We should all fall to our knees and kiss the ground we walk on. Gaea will know we are appreciating her. Be thankful that the Consciousness of God lives in us to create as He did and we can create methods to restore Gaea to health. We created our own Hell, so far. It's time to redecorate; spectating is out, participating is in.

In order to marshal forces to put an end to greed and misdirected power, we must not only describe John Lennon's ideal world, we must also agree on the cause for our actions. If you are interested in a couple of boards I created on Pinterest, click here.

New World Order

There are two possibilities for the New World Order – Government by the few or government by all. Since most of the population is ignorant about how to run the necessary affairs of society, the only answer for governance by all is to have a knowledge base available to all citizens. The only way to attain the ideal of John Lennon's "Imagine" is to create a system that serves the needs of each and every person on earth. That capability is available today, but requires the participation and cooperation of all who wish for that world to become reality.

The Plutarchy has many insidious ways of manipulating weak minds. Those minds are not the ones who will effect the change to create equality in society. It is up to mature minds to gather together in a unified front and let the weak minds follow. We need to form an "Occupy Earth" movement to take power away from the Plutarchy. It is not too late.

The Plutarchy works with fear and money to motivate the herds of sheep. Cheney and Bush destroyed the twin towers to create panic and start the war in Iraq. They used ignorance and patriotism to send young men to kill so they could have more money and our troops come home only to commit suicide for what they did. Is this the kind of World Order we want? When will we wake up and realize no one has power unless it is given to them? We have to stop giving up our power. It truly is that simple. We already know we cannot continue despoiling the planet, so all we need do is stop working for those who do. The Plutarchy hardly knows how to tie their shoelaces, much less how technology works. It is they who are ignorant of our power and we have to cut them off.

The first thing Occupy Earth must do is siphon money from the existing system. Open a Bank of Gaea and let all those who are concerned with the welfare of their children and grandchildren move their accounts into that bank. That will be the source of funding for the creation of interconnected communities that can separate themselves from the status quo. Start by rebuilding the small towns that have been neglected and begin the exodus from the putrid cities.

Connect the cyber-citizens through Internet communication and begin converting supply and demand systems to the Internet Cloud. Gather support from the technical world to divorce their skills from corporate allegiance to world peace. Once the system has been tested and proven, issue a declaration of dependence.

Declaration of Dependence

When in the Course of human events it becomes necessary for one people to dissolve the political bands which have connected them with another and to assume among the powers of the earth, the separate and equal station to which the Laws of Nature and of Nature's God entitle them, a decent respect to the opinions of mankind requires that they should declare the causes which impel them to the separation.

We hold these truths to be self-evident, that all men are created equal, that they are endowed by their Creator with certain unalienable rights; that among these are Life, Liberty and the pursuit of Happiness. — That to secure these rights, Governments are instituted among Men, deriving their just powers from the consent of the governed, — That whenever any Form of Government becomes destructive of these ends, it is the Right of the People to alter or to abolish it, and to institute new Government, laying its foundation on such principles and organizing its powers in such form, as to them shall seem most likely to effect their Safety and Happiness.

Prudence, indeed, will dictate that Governments long established should not be changed for light and transient causes; and accordingly all experience hath shown that mankind are more disposed to suffer, while evils are sufferable than to right themselves by abolishing the forms to which they are accustomed. But when a long train of abuses and usurpations, pursuing invariably the same Object evinces a design to reduce them under absolute Despotism, it is their right, it is their duty, to throw off such Government, and to provide new Guards for their future security. — Such has been the patient sufferance of these Colonies; and such is now the necessity which constrains them to alter their former systems of Government. The history of the present leadership is a history of repeated injuries and usurpations, all having in direct object the establishment of an absolute tyranny over our citizens. To prove this, let facts be submitted to a candid world.

The Plutarchy has refused its Assent to Laws, the most wholesome and necessary for the public good.

The Plutarchy has forbidden its Governors to pass Laws of immediate and pressing importance, unless suspended in their operation till its Assent should be obtained; and when so suspended, The Plutarchy has utterly neglected to attend to them.

The Plutarchy has refused to pass other Laws for the accommodation of large districts of people, unless those people would relinquish the right of Representation in the Legislature, a right inestimable to them and formidable to tyrants only.

The Plutarchy has called together legislative bodies at places unusual, uncomfortable, and distant from the depository of their Public Records, for the sole purpose of fatiguing them into compliance with its measures.

The Plutarchy has dissolved Representative Houses repeatedly, for opposing with manly firmness its invasions on the rights of the people.

The Plutarchy has refused for a long time, after such dissolutions, to cause others to be elected, whereby the Legislative Powers, incapable of Annihilation, have returned to the People at large for their exercise; the State remaining in the mean time exposed to all the dangers of invasion from without, and convulsions within.

The Plutarchy has obstructed the Administration of Justice by refusing its Assent to Laws for establishing Judiciary Powers.

The Plutarchy has made judges dependent on its Will alone for the tenure of their offices, and the amount and payment of their salaries.

The Plutarchy has erected a multitude of New Offices, and sent hither swarms of Officers to harass our people and eat out their substance.

The Plutarchy has kept among us, in times of peace, Standing Armies without the Consent of our legislatures.

The Plutarchy has affected to render the Military independent of and superior to the Civil Power.

The Plutarchy has combined with others to subject us to a jurisdiction foreign to our constitution, and unacknowledged by our laws; giving its Assent to their Acts of pretended Legislation:

For quartering large bodies of armed troops among us:

For protecting them, by a mock Trial from punishment for any murders which they should commit on the inhabitants of the earth:

For imposing taxes on us without our Consent:

For depriving us in many cases, of the benefit of trial by Jury:

For transporting us beyond seas to be tried for pretended offenses:

For taking away our charters, abolishing our most valuable laws and altering fundamentally the forms of our Governments:

For suspending our own Legislatures and declaring themselves invested with power to legislate for us in all cases whatsoever.

The Plutarchy has abdicated Government here, by declaring us out of its protection and waging war against us.

The Plutarchy has plundered our seas, ravaged our coasts, burnt our towns, and destroyed the lives of our people.

The Plutarchy is transporting large armies to complete the works of death, desolation, and tyranny, already begun with circumstances of Cruelty & Perfidy scarcely paralleled in the most barbarous ages, and totally unworthy of the Head of a civilized nation.

The Plutarchy has excited domestic insurrections amongst us, and has endeavored to bring on the inhabitants of planet and fomented undistinguished destruction of all ages, sexes and conditions.

In every stage of these oppressions we have petitioned for redress in the most humble terms: Our repeated Petitions have been answered only by repeated injury. Any leader, whose character is thus marked by every act which may define a tyrant, is unfit to be the ruler of a free people.

Nor have we been wanting in attentions to our political leaders. We have warned them from time to time of attempts by their legislature to extend an unwarrantable jurisdiction over us. We have appealed to their native justice and magnanimity, and we have conjured them by the ties of our common kindred to disavow these usurpations, which would inevitably interrupt our connections and correspondence. They too have been deaf to the voice of justice and of consanguinity. We must, therefore, acquiesce in the necessity, which denounces our separation, and hold them, as we hold the rest of mankind, enemies in war, in peace friends.

We, therefore, the representatives of Occupy Earth, appealing to the Supreme Judge of the world for the rectitude of our intentions, do, in the Name, and by Authority of the good People of all world citizens, solemnly publish and declare, that these united Communities are, and of right ought to be free and independent, that they are absolved from all allegiance to the Plutarchy, and that all political connection between them and the Occupy Earth State, is and ought to be totally dissolved; and that as Free and Independent States, they have full power to conclude peace, contract alliances, establish commerce, and to do all other acts and things which independent states may of right do. — And for the support of this Declaration, with a firm reliance on the protection of Divine Providence, we mutually pledge to each other our lives, our fortunes, and our sacred honor.

Of course, this is loosely adapted from the original, but the point should be clear. There is no reason to prevent issuing "world citizen" status to participants to supersede nationalism. Occupy Earth can be regarded as a "cyber-nation" independent from all other nations until it becomes the only nation. John Lennon would be pleased. Our grandchildren will be pleased that we saved them. They can live in communities like this:

www.ingramcontent.com/pod-product-compliance
Lightning Source LLC
Chambersburg PA
CBHW072247310526
45795CB00011B/318